AMAZING LOVE

AMAZING LOVE

True accounts of

God's transforming power

in the lives of

ordinary women

Tyndale House Publishers, Inc.
WHEATON, ILLINOIS

Visit Tyndale's exciting Web site at www.tyndale.com

Library of Congress Cataloging-in-Publication Data

Amazing love : true accounts of God's transforming power in the lives of ordinary women.
    p. cm.
  ISBN 0-8423-7076-5 (sc : alk. paper)
   1. Christian women—Biography. 2. Women in Christianity. 3. God—Love. I. Tyndale House Publishers.
BR1713.A53 1997
277.3′082′0922—dc20
                                             96-19074

Printed in the United States of America

02 01 00 99 98 97
10 9 8 7 6 5 4 3 2 1

CONTENTS

INTRODUCTION

I love to read a good story, don't you? A story has the power to make us laugh or cry. It sweeps us along as dramatic events unfold, compelling us to turn page after page to find out what happens. If we've faced a similar situation—or shared similar feelings—we empathize. We agonize when the person in the story is in pain; we rejoice when that person triumphs against all odds. And somehow our own burdens become more manageable. We can begin to move ahead confidently, with God's help, through our unique crises and disappointments.

The stories of *our* lives rarely are wrapped up neatly while we live in this world. Yet, as we live out our own stories, moment by moment, we discover something amazing: God gives us moments of grace! He grants us hope in our darkness, leads us toward healing, and even allows us—miraculously—to help others in *their* crises.

That's what *Amazing Love* is all about. It's a book of stories about *real* women, like you and me, who face difficult situations and incredible odds and yet can testify to God's grace in their moments of greatest need. Their stories are varied and gripping:

- A woman is raped and has to make a painful decision: whether or not to keep her baby.

- A woman lives with debilitating panic attacks.
- A woman is forced to choose between her love for God and a well-paying job.
- A woman's long search for her birth mother leads to more of a surprise than she bargained for.
- A woman discovers that her daughter is a lesbian.
- A woman struggles to love, understand, and honor her father.
- A woman's definition of forgiveness is tested when her husband has an affair.
- A woman is painfully aware of her infertility and longing for a child.
- A woman whose home is destroyed by fire feels the ache of loss.
- A woman works to "fall in love" again with her husband.
- A woman wonders if her faith can uphold her in a time of financial need.

These stories are more than just "a good read." They encourage us to look everywhere—in ourselves and in others—for those moments when God's grace enters our life and gives us hope. They uplift our faith in God.

And as we become more aware of our Lord's day-to-day working in our lives, may we develop, as Walter Wangerin Jr. says in his book *Ragman and Other Cries of Faith*, "Eyes, bright God, to see you everywhere . . . and ears, thou roll of thunder, and feeling for your presence."

Ramona Cramer Tucker

I Had to Fall in Love With My Husband . . . *Again*

C.C. BROOKS*

*The names in the article, including that of the author, have been changed for privacy.

When two caring people
who are committed to each
other wrestle with the
inevitable hard times that
confront every married couple
in a spirit of kindness and
tenderness and forgiveness,
miracles do happen.

Dale Evans Rogers

I greeted Valentine's Day with the usual mix of pain and dread. Shopping for a card with just the right amount of emotional detachment wasn't easy on this day meant for sweethearts. As I searched row after row of cards, reading romantic verse after romantic verse, I grew more depressed. Each sentiment painted a picture of what was missing in my marriage: intimacy.

It had been years since my husband, David, and I had been close. When I married David twenty years ago, I thought we'd grow together in every way—spiritually, emotionally, and physically. We would have children, go to church together, establish a loving Christian home—just like my parents.

David had told me he believed in God. He had attended church as a child and had sung in the youth choir. He'd even read the entire Bible twice—I certainly couldn't make that claim. But soon after our wedding, I discovered that David's Christianity lacked substance. Each Sunday, I ended up sitting in church alone.

There were other surprises, too. When David came home from work each day, I wanted to snuggle, but he wanted to eat. I wanted to chat, but he wanted to watch the news. I wanted kids, and although David didn't, he agreed to one child after the car loan was paid off. Three years later, though, an emergency hysterectomy dashed my hopes of motherhood.

Over the next ten years, David progressed in his career, and I found fulfillment in mine. While I was proud of my husband's success, the more he achieved, the less significant I felt. David's job became "the other woman," and he put it ahead of our marriage and even himself. Although I ached for David's attention, I couldn't mask the gnawing pain in my heart any longer. Frustration and anger spilled into almost every conversation. Secretly I blamed David and his job-centered priorities for all our troubles. But each time I tried to explain my needs, he took it as personal criticism and became angry and defensive.

Soon our parallel lives veered off sharply. Too many missed communications, chilly silences, and strings of unkind words led us even further apart, and we had even stopped making love.

Tears pooled in my eyes as I returned to my car empty-handed. Once home, I opened my Bible, and a verse bounced off the page, demanding attention: "Wives, in the same way be submissive to your husbands so that, if any of them do not believe the word, they may be won over without words by the behavior of their wives" (1 Pet. 3:1).

How am I supposed to win him over by my behavior when my anger is so close to the surface? I anguished. I knew God places a high value on the "unfading beauty of a gentle and quiet spirit" (1 Pet. 3:4), but my spirit was anything but gentle and quiet. Seething resentment simmered just below the surface, erupting into anger when circumstances turned up the heat.

But divorce wasn't an option. I couldn't separate what God had joined (Matt. 19:4-6). With our happiness hanging in the balance, I surrendered the matter to God. "Change me, Lord— I'll do whatever you ask."

Then came a clear impression. I sensed God saying, *Do what you did when you first dated David. Wear the same kind of clothes, make him Chicken Kiev, and . . . flirt.*

"Flirt with David, Lord?" I gasped. "He'll think I'm nuts!" I certainly didn't feel like flirting—those days were long gone. But I realized that David was worth it—*we* were worth it. Getting our lives back on the same track would take effort—and God had dropped the ball squarely in my court.

I thought back to when we were dating. Every other weekend, David had driven more than two hundred miles one way just to see me. We loved to picnic at a park near the university. The menu was always the same: apples, cheese, and a quart of chocolate milk. We'd sit under a gnarly oak tree and feast on love and laughter.

I glanced down at my shapeless cotton pants and oversized T-shirt—my standard uniform since I'd begun working at home. I couldn't remember the last time I wore something just for David. Comfort and practicality even dictated my sleeping attire—cool cotton nightgowns or old T-shirts.

I decided to fix myself up for David when he came home that evening. I slipped into a silky blue dress and put some music on the stereo, and when David opened the front door, I handed him a small grocery sack containing two shiny green apples, some smoky Gouda cheese, and a pint of low-fat chocolate milk. A twenty-seven-year-old grin flashed across the forty-seven-year-old face before me.

It was a start—but we were a long way from the carefree laughter we enjoyed at the beginning of our relationship. It would take a lot more than chocolate milk, a new look, and an old memory to warm the atmosphere in our marriage.

One by one, the Lord revealed other areas I had neglected by taking me back to those early years when we fell in love.

On one of our first dates, we went to the zoo and discovered some basic temperament differences. On more than one occasion, my calm and collected Connecticut Yankee asked me to cool it when I'd squeal with a little too much delight.

Had I cooled it so much over the years that I'd frozen all my laughter and joy inside? For the first time, I began seeing things from David's perspective. What I needed from him were the very things I'd been denying him: affection, consideration, kindness, acceptance, forgiveness, and love. In order to reap, I had to *sow*—first.

Daily the Lord showed me little ways to warm up the icy climate in our home—like celebrating David's half-birthday with half a cake, or bringing him a bouquet of flowers, or simply thanking him for going to work every day. Connecting through these old and new sights, smells, sounds, and tastes, we discovered new emotional intimacy. But touching—making that final sensory connection—scared me.

It had been two years since we'd made love. Seven times in a row I'd initiated lovemaking, only to be rejected. Now, in the midst of my fear, I felt the Lord's gentle leading: *Start at the beginning, like when you first met.*

Initially I began by standing closer to David, lightly grabbing his arm when we talked, or placing my hand on his back—anything to establish direct contact. After several days of "thawing," I made my move.

"David, I need a hug," I announced. Our first attempt was stiff, almost awkward. When he started to pull away, I held on and said, "I need more—at least sixty seconds." Embracing again, we began to get silly, squirming and leaning and pulling each other off balance. Soon we were laughing like a couple of kids. When we broke apart, I felt as if new life had been born into our union. I noticed David's face brighten, too.

Each day I asked for and received these revitalizing moments of warmth. Then one day, while I stood at the kitchen sink doing dishes, David tapped me from behind. I turned around to find his waiting arms, poised for a hug.

With all this touching and hugging going on, I knew where God was leading us—to the bedroom. Still uneasy about resuming our physical relationship, I prayed, "Lord, help me be the kind of wife David needs, the kind he desires. And give me a new desire for him as well."

Then one ordinary Saturday afternoon, David grabbed my hand and looked at me with tender, pleading eyes. As we embraced, forgiveness melted our hearts. Apprehensions, awkwardness, and all the old hurts vanished in a moment. The timing, the place, the circumstance—all had been orchestrated by God. We came together as naturally and comfortably as when we were first married and completed the final step in our journey back to each other.

Yes, we still have struggles. David doesn't yet know the Lord, and at times I fail to speak lovingly or behave in a manner worthy of Jesus' name. But God is doing a work in me, and he has promised to complete it (Phil. 1:6). I enjoy finding new ways to please my husband, like watching a football game with him, surprising him with a special meal on a ho-hum Tuesday, or buying him a balloon just to say "I love you."

God is working in David, too. He has changed—in his conversation, his attitudes, his tenderness toward me. David often does the dishes or grocery shopping when he sees I've had a difficult day. Sometimes he whisks me away for a special treat, always keeping our destination a surprise. As we draw closer to each other, God is drawing David closer to himself.

As I continue to walk in obedience to God's Word, I need not worry, knowing he will provide everything I need—including a loving husband (Matt. 6:33). Now when I search the racks for a romantic valentine, the only tears I shed are tears of joy. As I choose the perfect expression of my love, I realize just how far we've come.

And each time David taps me on the shoulder for a hug at the kitchen sink, I breathe a quick thanks to the One who is doing it all.

My Daughter Was Conceived in Rape

ANGIE BLOEDORN
as told to UNA MCMANUS

I have decided to stick with love. Hate is too great a burden to bear.

Martin Luther King Jr.

C ongratulations! You're pregnant!"
       Three times in the past I'd heard those words—and
       each time, my heart had overflowed with happiness.
But on that cold February day, when I heard the nurse's
announcement, I fell into my husband's arms and sobbed
uncontrollably.

In a voice choked with tears, I cried to Wally, "What am I
going to do?" His face was stunned, ashen, but he comforted
me: "You're going to have a baby."

We both knew Wally wasn't the father of this baby. After our
third child was born, Wally had had a vasectomy. The father
of this baby was a criminal—a dirty, foul-smelling man who
had broken into my car and brutally raped me.

I shuddered, remembering the terror of that night.

It had happened in the parking lot after a shopping trip to
the mall. I never saw the rapist's face because everything
happened too fast. Afterward, my shame was so great that I
didn't go to the police. I walked around in shock, more dead
than alive, until Wally, worried, questioned me.

"Something is terribly wrong, Angie," he said. "I can tell by
your face. Tell me what's bothering you. There's nothing so
bad that we can't face it together."

Finally, after much coaxing, I blurted out the whole horrible story. Wally's eyes filled with tears. "Angie, why didn't you tell me?" he cried as he gathered me into his arms. "You didn't have to bear this burden alone."

Somehow we got through the holidays, but in January my period, punctual as clockwork, didn't come. And in February, Wally went along with me to the doctor for a pregnancy test.

Now my worst nightmare had come true—and I wanted to die. "Angie, you don't have to go through with this pregnancy," my gynecologist said. "I can perform an abortion in my office. Then you can get on with your life."

It sounded so easy. But I heard myself say to the doctor, "I can't do that! This baby is my baby, too! I can't get rid of it just because of what its father did."

Wally agreed. "I'll love this baby as if it were my own," he assured me. "You know why? Because I love you—and this little baby is a part of you, no matter who the father is."

But Wally and I seemed to be the only ones who wanted me to have the baby. Even my own sister offered me no support, advising me to "get rid of the problem." My mother warned me that I'd be reminded of the rapist every time I looked at my baby. They made me furious because they carried on as if my baby were some kind of evil clone of her father—and not a part of me as well.

The more the whole world advised against it, the fiercer my love for the innocent baby became—and the stronger I grew in my resolve to give birth to this child. Because of my extended family's lack of support, I turned to our local crisis pregnancy center and there found friends who gave me the emotional support and encouragement I needed in my decision.

Although I was thankful for Wally's love and understanding, deep in my heart I doubted he could love this child. Adoption seemed to be the best option. Yet as the baby grew inside me, I became more attached to her—I was sure it was a girl. I decided to name her Hannah, which means "grace." Daily I prayed I'd somehow have God's grace to turn this tragedy into joy. At night, I would stroke my bulging tummy and whisper to Hannah, "Little baby, some people think you shouldn't be allowed to live. But I can hardly wait to see you and to hold you. I love you, little girl." As my love for Hannah grew, I felt my prayers were being answered.

My labor lasted sixteen hours. The last three hours, I cried and cried. As I pushed her out of my body, I felt as if I were releasing all the pain of the past nine months.

The doctor who'd advised me to get an abortion was crying, too, as she handed Hannah over to me. "She's lovely, Angie," she said huskily. "I'm so sorry I suggested you abort her."

It was apparent right away that Hannah wasn't Caucasian. She has dark skin and dark brown hair. All my other children are blond. I had considered the possibility of Hannah's being biracial since I hadn't seen the rapist's face. And I'd been concerned that, if she were, life would be harder for her. But now, all that didn't matter. All that mattered was the precious baby I held in my arms.

Hannah is now five, and she's brought our family much joy. She's healthy, and fortunately, neither one of us has tested positive for HIV. Because she's the "baby" of the family, Hannah gets lots of attention. She loves to sing—nursery rhymes, songs from church or the radio—she's very dramatic and verbal.

I decided I'd tell Hannah about her situation by comparing Wally to Joseph, Jesus' earthly father. "That Joseph was quite a guy," I told her after we read the Christmas story together. "Jesus wasn't his real child, but he loved Jesus as if he were. You know, your daddy's a lot like Joseph—he's not your biological father, but he loves you just like you're his." I don't look forward to the day I have to tell Hannah the details about her conception. I know it won't be easy, but no matter how I do it, I'll tell her we love her and that's all that matters.

I believe there's a special reason for Hannah to have been born. She's already changed lives. My relatives used to be prejudiced. But they look at this precious child—and they love her! And Wally's grown from a passive parent into a more involved father. We've grown closer as a couple. I believe God is honoring us for the decision we made.

I want Hannah to know that I don't see her as a tragic accident. God has a plan for her, despite how her life began. Through this whole experience, I've learned that God can bring good out of the most horrible situation—even something as terrible as rape.

Up in Flames

KAY MARSHALL STROM

*The best challenges force you
to identify yourself.*

Chaim Potok

W e were in Oxford, England, when we got the news about our house.

"There's been a terrible fire here in Santa Barbara," a friend told me over the crackling phone connection. "Your house has burned."

"Burned?" I asked numbly. "What do you mean, burned?"

"It was destroyed," he said.

"Go up there today," I told him. "Save everything you can before looters get in."

"Kay," he said firmly, "there is nothing to save. *Nothing.* Everything is gone."

Gone? Everything? All our family pictures? My daughter's art portfolio? My grandfather's Bible? My son's photography? My great-grandmother-in-law's silver? The screenplay I'd almost finished after three years of work? My collection of stuffed lambs? The furniture my husband built? *Everything?*

By the time I hung up the phone, my husband, Larry, and our kids knew what had happened. None of us felt much like talking. Silently we put our arms around each other and held tight.

That was the beginning of our tears. Still holding on to each other, we went back to our room to cry and try to comprehend our loss.

Our trip to England was to have been one great last hurrah. Now that our children were almost grown, we knew this would likely be our last trip together. We had saved for it for two years. And we had had a great time. Now, three days before we were to return home, we got this phone call. Suddenly our happy vacation spirit was gone. In its place was a stunned sense of doubt and dread.

"You know what?" our son, Eric, said. "This guest house in England is the closest thing we have to a home."

What a depressing thought!

Later that evening we all sat around a small table in our room and took the photos out of our wallets. Carefully, tenderly, we spread them out to see what we had left.

"Oh, look!" I exclaimed. "Here's that picture of you kids dressed up in Civil War era costumes!"

"Here's your first prom, Lisa," Eric said. "I didn't know I had that."

"Look at this one of you, Eric," Larry said. "You're missing your two front teeth!"

"Recognize this?" Lisa asked me. "It's you and Dad on a big date in college."

"Where did you get that?" I asked in amazement.

"Out of the picture drawer. I thought it was cute, so I put it in my wallet."

Our little pile of photographs brought back a flood of memories. We talked together long into the night, reminiscing about trips. Friends. Pets. Birthday parties. And all those wonderful Christmas mornings.

Nothing prepared us for getting back to Santa Barbara. Our neighborhood was devastated. Tears sprang to our eyes as we looked down the hill where 105 homes had once stood. Now we could count only eight. Everywhere we looked we saw charred ruins, blackened chimneys, burned-out cars, ashes.

"It looks like it was bombed," Larry gasped.

Were it not for the charred bedsprings and a doubled-over refrigerator, we wouldn't have been able to tell one room from the next.

"Everyone go through the ashes," I said. "There has to be something here."

We desperately searched and searched but found nothing. Then, just when I was ready to quit, I saw something lying among the ashes of what had been our china cabinet. If I didn't know better I would have thought it was a piece of carefully crafted modern art. Melted to a pair of turkey-shaped salt and pepper shakers was the base of a silver candlestick Larry and I had received as a wedding present. Cemented to its side was a melted cup we bought on a family vacation. Firmly affixed to the left side were Lisa's baby fork and spoon, and across its right was Eric's long-handled baby spoon.

"It's a summary of our life," I said in wonder. Just like the memorial stones Joshua had the Israelites take over into the Promised Land after God miraculously divided the waters of the Jordan River, this melted collage would always be a remembrance for us.

Yesterday a friend told me, "I just can't believe God would allow you to lose your home."

Again and again I had echoed those same words: *Why, God? Why did you allow our home to be taken away from us?*

Suddenly, after all my questions, after all my doubts, God gave me an answer. We hadn't lost our home at all. All we had lost was our house.

Today our home is in a rented condominium. Last month it was in a borrowed house. Over Christmas it was in a friend's mother-in-law's mobile home. Our home is wherever our family is. It's the place where we sit together and remember and laugh and drink hot chocolate and play Monopoly. It's where we pray together and remember God's blessings to us.

I want to understand God's reasons for allowing things to happen, to comprehend his timing. But most often I don't understand. Yet always, in every situation, God is in charge. Whatever happens, I am his child, safe in his keeping.

Our house is gone. Where we once ate and slept, practiced the piano and baked cookies, played games and opened Christmas gifts, nothing remains but a bare dirt lot. But our home? That we carry with us.

In Search of My
Birth Mother

SHERRIE ELDRIDGE

How often we look upon
God as our last and feeblest
resource! We go to him
because we have nowhere else
to go. And then we learn that
the storms of life have driven
us, not upon the rocks, but
into the desired haven.

George MacDonald

I always knew I was adopted. My parents broke the news when I was just old enough to understand: "We chose you out of all the babies in the world to be ours."

Even though my adoptive parents tried to make me feel special, unanswered questions about my adoption kept surfacing within me. As a young girl, people always asked about my nationality because I looked so different from the rest of my family. "I don't know," I would say. "I was adopted."

My late teen years were especially turbulent. Conflicts with my adoptive mother were common. I often wondered if my birth mother would be as hard to get along with.

I married and soon started my own family. Throughout my pregnancy with my second child, thoughts of my birth mother pressed in upon me. *What kind of woman was she? Why did she give me up? How could a woman carry a baby for nine months, experience the miracle of birth, and not think about that child for the rest of her life?* I wanted to find her and let her know I was happy.

Then, when I was twenty-seven, I turned my life over to Christ. But it wasn't until two or three years later, as my walk with God grew, that I connected the issue of my adoption with God's sovereignty. I read in Psalm 139 how I was "fearfully and wonderfully made" and that "all the days ordained for me were written in your book before one of them came to be." God had chosen my adoptive parents for me—he really was in control! Yet with each birthday that passed, I still thought about my birth mother—and wondered if she thought about me.

But it wasn't until five years ago, after my adoptive parents had died, that I decided to search for her. I struggled inwardly with my motives, wanting to make sure they were pleasing to God. Initially, my husband wasn't in favor of my search—he was afraid I would be hurt. Other extended family members chided me for wanting to open a "can of worms." Despite my family's opposition, my desire to find my mother only increased. One Sunday, my pastor spoke on Ecclesiastes 3: "There is a time for everything . . . a time to search and a time to give up." That phrase "a time to search" stood out. After much prayer and counsel, I was convinced that my desire was God-given—and that this was *my* time to search.

Before her death, my adoptive mother had left some clues behind: my birth mother's last name and place of residence at the time of my birth. I hired a professional to aid in my search and, before long, received additional information by obtaining my sealed birth certificate.

A few months later, I traveled to my home state to work intensively with the adoption worker. After two days of combing city directories and state library and health department records, we learned which state my birth mother resided in. I felt numb with disbelief! My birth mother was no longer a fantasy but a real person with an address and phone number!

The adoption worker paved the way by making the initial call. "What do you want me to tell her?" she asked.

"Tell her I'm married, have two grown daughters, and am back in college full-time. Ask her about her nationality, who my father was, and her medical history." Then the Holy Spirit prompted me to add, "Tell her, 'Thank you for giving me life.'"

I waited nearly two hours at home while she talked with my birth mother. Finally, the adoption worker called back. "Was it good or bad?" I asked eagerly.

"Both," she said. "Your mother wants you to know she is a woman you can be proud of, but she doesn't want to talk about your father because you were conceived in rape."

I was stunned! I had never considered rape as the reason my birth mother gave me up for adoption. My heart sank.

"She sounds just like you," the adoption worker added. As she spoke, her call waiting suddenly clicked in. "I bet that's your mom. Hold on!" After what seemed like an eternity, she said, "Sure enough! It's your mom, and she wants you to call."

My hands trembled as I pushed the buttons. A gentle-sounding voice said, "Hello."

"Catherine,* this is Sherrie, your daughter. I never thought this moment would come!"

Our first conversation lasted into the wee hours of the night. We agreed to exchange photos and began thinking about a possible reunion. For the remainder of that night, I lay sleepless in bed, pondering the turn of events. Suddenly, I had a new family: a mother, a half sister, and a half brother. As morning dawned, so did feelings of peace and completeness. While I still had unanswered questions about my father, I now had a history! First Corinthians 2:9 came to mind: "No eye has seen, no ear has heard, no mind has conceived what God has prepared for those who love him."

Within days, my birth mother and I had planned a reunion to be held in two weeks. We exchanged photos, and in a subsequent conversation, she told me, "When I look at your sweet face, I know you are mine." She told me she had pur-

*Her name has been changed for privacy.

25

chased a diamond-studded gold pin for me, and I compiled a photo album for her. We finalized plans for our reunion.

As the plane lifted away from the airport, emotion engulfed me. I had always believed God loved me, but on this particular day, his personal touch was unmistakable! That he would reunite me with my birth mother was beyond my wildest dreams!

My birth mother, half sister, and stepsister met me as I walked off the plane. When I saw her run to me with arms outstretched, it was a moment like none other. Some adoptees refer to it as the moment of birth. I vacillated between laughter and tears. As is common during reunions, I couldn't stop staring at her. The resemblance between us was remarkable. My self-esteem took a giant leap. I didn't feel "different" anymore.

The first night we talked, I learned my mother had lost another baby two years after I was born. She told me she had wondered if God were punishing her for giving me up. Although I tried to stay sensitive to my birth mother's wishes and avoided asking her about my father or the circumstances of my conception, as our visit progressed, our budding relationship became increasingly strained. When I gave her my photo album, I thought it would be an opportunity for me to tell her about my life. Up until that time, she had asked next to nothing about me. But she quickly thumbed through the pages and put it away, saying politely, "Thank you very much." Later that afternoon, she said, "This is going too fast for me. I've had it."

"What do you mean?" I asked, biting my cheek as my bottom lip began to quiver.

"This is very difficult for me," she said. "You don't know what a pressure this has been on me."

By the last morning of our visit, I felt uncomfortable leaving the photo album with her. As we drove to the airport, I asked her if she would like me to take it back home. That triggered a well of emotion for her, and she blurted out, "You don't know how much you have hurt me. You don't know how hard it is to give up a baby. There wasn't a day that I didn't think about you."

I could feel warm tears streaming from my eyes. I reached into my purse for a tissue. By the time I boarded my return flight, we were both exhausted. "I love you, Catherine," I said, "and I'm glad you're my mom."

"I love you, too," she responded, her eyes welling with tears.

Two days after returning home, I sat in church and listened to our pastor preach on how the presence of Christ in a believer's life often brings division between family members. After church, my husband waited patiently as I went from friend to friend, telling them my wonderful reunion story and showing them the gold pin my birth mother had given me. Later that afternoon, I called to thank her again for the visit.

"I just called to tell you I think you're wonderful and that I had a great time at your home last week."

"Thank you," she said, her voice flat and emotionless. Suddenly I had the sick feeling that something was wrong. By the end of the conversation, she announced she wanted nothing further to do with me. I was stunned and crushed.

Despite the anguish I felt at this turn of events, I later realized that because Christ had endured the ultimate rejection for me—his death on the cross—his strength could carry me through the loss of a relationship with my birth mother. While I had been on the telephone with Catherine, Jesus had stood with me, making his presence known. As his child, I was intimately united with him—and *he* would never leave me or forsake me. At that moment, the words of Isaiah 49:15 comforted me: "Can a mother forget the baby at her breast and have no compassion on the child she has borne? Though she may forget, I will not forget you!" God felt that way about *me*.

Reunion with a child given up for adoption—especially one conceived in rape—can send a birth mother into a grief process that has been long repressed. Suddenly my birth mother not only had to deal with meeting the child she had given up—but also with the pain of reliving the circumstances of my conception.

Within a few days, I wrote a letter to Catherine, thanking her once again for giving me the gift of life forty-seven years ago—and for letting me back into her life, if only for a short time. I affirmed my desire for a friendship with her and invited her to reestablish contact with me. That was eight months ago. As yet, I have heard nothing back from her.

As I look back on my search, many things come into focus. First, I needed to face the pain of my past so I could live fully in the present. As an adoptee, I was subconsciously searching for the mother I had lost at birth. For me, never knowing her would be far worse than knowing her and being rejected. Finding her put a missing piece of my puzzle into place.

I also saw vividly how God is able to bring good out of any situation for his children, and the good he brought out of this was *me*. I know there are no mistakes, no illegitimate children, in God's kingdom. I am his child, and he planned my life, even though my birth parents didn't. My heavenly Father knew all along what was best for me and, in his protective love, removed me from an undesirable situation.

But was God unfaithful in keeping the promise from 1 Corinthians 2:9 he had given me the morning after I found her? At the time, I thought that verse applied to my future relationship with my birth mother. While that vision has died, in its place has come something far better—a deeper union with Jesus.

At times, it seems that all that's left of my relationship with Catherine is the little gold pin she gave me. But in reality there's much more: her warm smile; her gentle, soothing voice; the way she tilts her head; the squared jaw; the tiny earlobes. Even though she put me out of her life, no matter where I go, whenever I look into the mirror I see a reflection of her.

My forty-seven-year search is now over. It ended, not in the arms of my birth mother, as I had expected, but at the feet of my Savior. For this, I will always be grateful.

Honoring My Father

JOYCE CAVANO*

*The names in this article, including that of the author, have been changed for privacy.

*Reconciliation is not
weakness or cowardice. It
demands courage, nobility,
generosity—an overcoming of
oneself rather than one's
adversary.*

Pope Paul VI

S and castles remind me most of him. My father helped me build sand castles on the endless beaches of Cape Cod, and no seven-year-old girl felt more proud. Locking me in a big bear hug, Dad complimented me on my awkward creations and called me his favorite artist.

That was our last vacation together. I now look at photographs of a father and daughter sharing sweet moments and wonder what might have been.

Ours appeared to be the picture-perfect suburban family of the midsixties. My father had a prestigious job in aerospace engineering, and Mom, like most mothers of the era, stayed at home to care for her five children. We shared meals together and attended church every Sunday. My parents were well known in our community; we kids were happy and loved.

But Dad drank. That seemed to be the price to pay for being in my parents' circle of friends. Although we were regular churchgoers, at the many parties Mom and Dad gave I heard raucous laughter and the name of Jesus taken in vain. Jesus Christ was nothing more than a swear word to these people, while the beer would pour and pour.

Soon after we returned from Cape Cod, I heard a terrible

argument between Mom and Dad. They'd never before raised their voices at each other. But this particular Saturday morning, I couldn't hear the cartoons on television because of the shouting upstairs. I plainly heard accusatory words like "affair" from my mother and "lunatic" from my father. For countless nights afterward, my sister, two brothers, and I grew accustomed to having our sleep interrupted by shouts and slamming doors.

My father began spending less time at home, so when I got the chance, I'd go anywhere to be with him. Once he stopped at the house of a female acquaintance, and while I waited for him in the living room, I played with the woman's daughter, rolling a ball back and forth with her. When I retrieved the ball in the dining room, I discovered my father locked in an embrace with the woman! When I told Mom about it the next day, she in turn confronted Dad. He then confronted me. I'll never forget my father's trembling hand and the venom in his voice. "You didn't see anything," he whispered, seething. "We're going to have to put you in a mental hospital because you're crazy." My own father threatened me because I told the truth!

My parents' horrible verbal matches soon escalated into physical assaults. Once, Dad attempted to hit Mom with a beer bottle. As he lowered his arm to strike her head, my sister, Susan*, intervened and was struck instead. Mom rushed her to the hospital emergency room, and as soon as my mother told the nurse what had happened, Dad burst through the door. "She did it!" he yelled, pointing at Mom.

Dad moved out of the house a few days later. Within two years, my parents were divorced. Divorce was uncommon in our suburban neighborhood. After playing at my house one Saturday, a friend quietly asked me if I had a father, since she hadn't seen him all day. I looked down at my feet as I stammered that my dad didn't live with us anymore. I was too ashamed to have that girl come to my house again. Not only had my father moved out, he had moved hundreds of miles away to Arizona. I felt abandoned and unloved.

The distance between my parents was fine with Mom. By then, she truly hated her estranged husband—and she did all she could to make us feel the same way. My father's actions certainly didn't soften our feelings toward him. It wasn't long before Dad stopped sending the court-ordered weekly child support payments, and the courts could not—or would not—do anything about it. Mom, my sister, my brothers, and I lived on food and clothing provided by neighbors. Sometimes we had only tomato soup for breakfast and potatoes for dinner. We used to hide upstairs when bill collectors knocked at the front door. Eventually, because Dad didn't make the mortgage payments, the house in which we lived was taken from us. I wondered how the father who had once seemed so caring could have become so cruel.

I vividly remember one night before my father moved away. Dad came to the front door, drunk. A terrible thunderstorm knocked a tree onto our house, electrical wires were down, and the streets were flooded. Mom was visibly upset, but Dad taunted her, making her cry. My sister, Susan, demanded that he stop tormenting Mom. "Young lady, the Bible says to 'honor your father,'" he retorted. "You are disobeying God by the way you speak to me."

Honor your father. As I reflect on those words, they affect me as much today as they did that stormy evening. How could I honor such a man? My father neglected our physical needs and hurt us emotionally. He not only lied about my mother, telling the neighbors she needed to be placed in an institution, he terrified me with the same threat. The man with whom I'd created sandcastles and dreams dashed both.

For the next twenty years of my life, except for hastily scribbled thank-yous for the birthday and holiday presents Dad would send, I had no real contact with my father.

Whether due to poor self-esteem, a need for love, or both, in my twenties I had a string of broken relationships with men. I so longed to be nurtured that I became promiscuous. Looking for security and happiness, I quit job after job. I was constantly anxious and depressed, believing I was too far gone for salvation.

Then, while in my midtwenties, I heard about a spiritual renewal program at a neighborhood church. There I heard Christians talk about Jesus' passionate love for them. I longed for their serenity and contentment in the Lord, their assurance that they were loved unconditionally by him. Somehow, in my youth, I'd come to believe God could love me only if I were perfect. Yet these wonderful Christians described a God who loved them—faults and all—and I found hope at last.

I sought a Christian therapist to help me work through the hurts of my past. But not long into the process, my therapist advised me that my healing wouldn't be complete without a reconciliation with my father. After twenty years of despising my dad, I was being instructed not only to forgive him but to reestablish a relationship with him!

At the time, one of my brothers had a polite relationship with Dad and gave me his phone number. He told my father I'd be calling. After a few days of trying to talk myself out of this reconciliation, I called, and Dad offered to pay my round-trip airfare for a reunion in Phoenix over the approaching Labor Day weekend. With conflicting feelings of fear and exhilaration, skepticism and hope, I made arrangements to meet a man who'd be waiting at my arrival gate wearing a Cleveland Indians baseball cap. A man who was my father.

I questioned, accused, shouted at, and cried with Dad over that long weekend. My father said Mom had been ungrateful for the life he'd provided for her, that she complained about him to friends and neighbors. He told me Mom was suspicious of his every female acquaintance, convinced he was having affairs with other women. Dad apologized for having told me so many years before that I should be institutionalized, yet he vehemently denied he'd had an affair with the woman I'd seen him embrace. He did admit to having had an affair with someone else, feeling unloved by Mom. Finally, Dad explained he hadn't been able to stand to be near Mom any longer, even though it meant leaving his children.

As is often the case, there's his side, her side, and the truth—and I don't think I'll know the latter in this lifetime. During that Labor Day weekend, my father confessed he'd recently been hospitalized with a long-standing addiction to alcohol, and his doctor said many years of alcohol abuse have affected his memory.

One weekend doesn't erase years of hurt, and forgiveness doesn't involve ignoring pain. But I now feel compassion for Dad, a compassion that comes only from the love of Jesus Christ.

My mother is angry that I've opened the lines of communication with my father. She says I'm foolish in my attempts to build this relationship with him. She suffers from the chronic bitterness that nearly destroyed me. I've told Mom about my personal relationship with the Lord, and I pray that her heart will change.

Dad's estrangement from my mother and siblings has left him a very lonely man. Yet my father says God is his constant companion, and he looks forward to going to church every Sunday. Beyond that, Dad is reticent to discuss his spiritual life, although he affirms my personal relationship with Jesus rather than scorning it as does my mother.

Dad still has his struggles with alcoholism. Many times he'd rather stay home than attend Alcoholics Anonymous. Sometimes his craving for beer gets the better of him, and I play the part of parent by long-distance telephone, demanding he seek professional help. But my father is aware of his failings, and that humility makes him kind and patient with others. He prayed for Mom when she was recently hospitalized, knowing she won't reciprocate such generosity. It's now been ten years of phone calls and letters between Dad and me. I wish I could say we have a warm relationship, but I can't. The rift between us is still in need of repair. Sometimes the man I call "Dad" seems to be a loving but distant uncle rather than a father. I'm still getting to know the man who remembers reading bedtime stories to his little daughter, memories I've lost over time. My father played no part in all the special events of my youth—my first date, prom, high school and college graduations. I often long for the lost years of my past and find myself resenting him for leaving. On those difficult occasions when he has been drinking, I find it frustrating to deal with him and wish he could parent *me* instead. Yet in these trying moments, I remember the mercy God has shown me for my sins, and the need to forgive.

Dad and I will never again share those simple, idyllic moments of building sand castles together. But with the love of Jesus Christ, I'm building a relationship with my father on something more stable than sand.

The Day after
Father's Day

DEBRA M. CRAIG
as told to MARIAN V. LIAUTAUD

*When I mourn I am filled
with pain that seems
unbearable at first. Sometimes
it turns to tears, and
sometimes to quiet moments
of reflection. It doesn't matter
which. The important thing is
that I am made vulnerable,
receptive—to more pain?
Perhaps, but certainly to God's
healing love. And Jesus makes
the pain bearable and the loss
understandable.*

Colleen Townsend Evans

My husband, Lee, kissed me good-bye as he left for work the Monday after Father's Day. Later that morning, he called to say he'd be home for lunch, anticipating the usual peanut-butter-and-jelly sandwich and *Perry Mason* rerun. But at 10:40 A.M., an irate customer stormed into the Jacksonville, Florida, GMAC (General Motors Acceptance Corporation) office where Lee worked. With a semiautomatic rifle in one hand and a handgun in the other, the man opened fire. After randomly shooting two customers and twelve employees, he finally turned the gun on himself.

When the rescue team found Lee, he was unconscious but alive. They pulled him away from a female coworker he had tried to save and discovered that five bullets had entered his body. The paramedics immediately began CPR on Lee, and when he regained consciousness, his first words were, "Help her. I'm OK."

As soon as I learned of the shooting, I rushed to Lee's office. A friend drove me to the hospital, but Lee was already on the operating table by the time we got there. I kept praying, but all I could think was, *God, please.*

While the surgeons worked on Lee, I went into a bathroom stall, got down on my knees, and started to bargain with God. I told him that if he let Lee live, I would never miss my daily prayer time again. A friend came in and told me the doctor wanted to see me. "I'm sorry," the doctor said. "The wounds were lethal."

When I pulled into our driveway at home, our children—Josh, eight, and Melissa, six—came running up to the car. "Is he dead?" Josh asked. "He's dead, isn't he?"

"Yes, he is," I said.

Then Melissa grabbed me and cried, "What will we do for food?"

I didn't sleep well that first night. Every time I rolled over, all I could think was *Lee is dead. Lee is dead.* I got up and opened the bag of Lee's belongings the hospital had given me. Inside were his pants, his socks, and the new wing-tip shoes we had given him for Father's Day. When I unrolled Lee's blood-soaked pants, I saw the bullet holes. Clutching his pants to my chest, I sobbed in grief. I couldn't imagine how we would make it without him.

In the months following Lee's death, I clung to God's Word for my own sense of peace and to reassure the children. Psalm 37:7 seemed to speak directly to us: "Be still before the Lord and wait patiently for him; do not fret when men succeed in their ways, when they carry out their wicked schemes." Verse 8 went on to say: "Refrain from anger and turn from wrath; do not fret—it leads only to evil." I realized that I had to forgive the man who had murdered my husband and trust in God's promise in verse 9: "For evil men will be cut off, but those who hope in the Lord will inherit the land."

God's Word also helped my children overcome their fears and sadness over losing their daddy. For Melissa's worries about our food and care, we looked to Psalm 37:25: "I have never seen the righteous forsaken or their children begging bread." Gradually, she came to know what it meant to trust in God's provision for us.

Josh feared for our protection. We had never been alone at night before, so I told him that God promises to defend widows and orphans against anyone taking advantage of them (Exod. 22:22-24).

Though God's promises helped us in very real ways, we still had to work through our grief and anger. Josh and Melissa asked me, "Why didn't Daddy run? Didn't he think about us?" I tried to help them understand that Lee never left anyone who needed help, just as he never left us in need. That's something we can be proud of.

It's so easy to say, yet harder to live, "In everything give thanks" (1 Thess. 5:18, NASB). I remember thanking God for our families and special friends, without whom we could not have survived the countless tasks of beginning again.

The children and I moved back to Macon, Georgia, where Lee and I had grown up, and I struggled with the burden of setting up a new house. The week before we moved in, I painted some of the rooms. Several times I had to climb down from the ladder to cry. I was filled with anguish over leaving the life I had with Lee behind. Then I sensed God saying, *Debra, Lee will never come down this hallway. He will never tuck the children into bed. There is nothing you can give him now that he doesn't already have with me. I have closed the door to this chapter in your life. All of your standing and knocking will not open it. You can choose to stand here in this grief and pain, or you can turn the corner and see what I have in store for you. Debra, you only have to live through today; just finish today.*

His words stung, but they challenged me to try to make a new life for myself and my children. Many times after that, when my pain felt unending, I remembered those words. Gradually I began to make new friends, and we became acclimated in our new church.

There is a season to mourn. The world is unpredictable, and

sometimes things happen beyond our control. But I've learned that our response to trouble must remain firm. No matter what the circumstances, we can put our trust in Jesus. There is also a season to begin again. As Psalm 23 says, "though I walk through the valley of the shadow of death," God promises to restore my soul. We cherish our memories, but just as spring brings new life to the earth, the children and I are coming to life again, too.

Forced to Choose

LINDA RIOS BROOK
as told to DIANE EBLE

Whoever is on God's side is
on the winning side and
cannot lose; whoever is on the
other side is on the losing side
and cannot win. Here there is
no chance, no gamble. There
is freedom to choose which
side we shall be on, but no
freedom to negotiate the
results of the choice once
it is made.

A. W. Tozer

My secretary walked into my office and silently handed me a copy of the latest *City Pages*, the local tabloid. "About a hundred of these were dropped off at the station," she said sympathetically, then left. Emblazoned across its front page was a photo of me before a microphone. Inside, an article caricatured my weekend activities—speaking at Christian gatherings and teaching Bible classes at my church—as suspect, even dangerous. The reporter raised questions about my influence, as general manager and president of KARE-TV in Minneapolis, on the television station's news coverage and the possibility that my Christian faith was biasing my hiring practices.

This was not the first time a newspaper had sniped at my faith. For the last ten of my twenty years in broadcasting, I have often been the only Christian in this secular arena. But ever since I had come to Minneapolis, my Christian activities had been a topic of conversation. I never understood why anyone would care about what I did in my spare time! Speaking in churches and teaching Bible classes were as much a part of me as the color of my eyes—it was work I believed God wanted me to do. Yet as a seasoned professional, I also knew how to keep my faith from interfering with the workplace or from forcing it on people who were disinterested in Christ.

But none of the other articles even compared to this story. There are no words to describe how I felt. Shock, disbelief, outrage—all were too mild. Violated was more like it! With such an unexpected, devastatingly public attack, what was I supposed to do?

Many of my employees wrote letters to a local newspaper, stating that I had never exerted religious influence on them or on the news operation. The incident sparked letters from the community, which were printed on the editorial pages of local newspapers. I even received hundreds of letters of support at my home.

Despite the hoopla, however, I never dreamed a tabloid article could cause my career to be on the line. But a couple of weeks later, I was called into the CEO's office and told, "You can't teach a Bible class or speak to Christian groups anymore. Choose what you think is most important to you. By the way, you're doing a great job with the station." End of meeting.

At first I thought, *I couldn't have heard right. Surely he isn't really telling me I can't do what I want on my own time!* But I soon learned that was *exactly* what the company was telling me. The realization hit me like a bombshell.

You don't give up a well-paying job without thinking and praying very hard about it—especially if your husband's job is *also* about to be eliminated due to corporate restructuring, your son attends a private Christian college, your daughter is in high school, and you have no other job prospects on the horizon. But to quit teaching and speaking about your faith in Christ—that is unspeakable!

I sought the counsel of three different pastors, and each told me he felt God had brought me to a point where I had to make a very public choice about what I truly believed. After much agony and prayer, I concluded they were right. For whatever reason, my faith had become a public issue. How could I say

I believed in God, then give up teaching about him just so I could keep a job? There was no choice for me: I had to resign. People have called me courageous, but I don't think it's that at all. Courage is about taking a risk when you don't know how things will turn out. I made my decision knowing I would suffer humiliation, grief, and depression. And I did. But I also knew I was dealing with the living God, and that whatever happened, it would turn out to be good.

So I resigned. Many people, including my family, thought I should sue my company and the tabloid. But as I thought and prayed about how to respond, I decided not to press suit. First of all, what would I gain? If I won and they were forced to take me back, where would I be? The company had not stood by me when they could have and should have. They chose not to. So why should I want to go back and work for them?

Second, the only time Christians get national attention, unfortunately, is when they've either done something illegal or they're in court. I didn't want to perpetuate that stereotype. I'd had enough of a taste of what the secular media can do with Christians. And my story had already gained national attention. What more could I say that would add anything? Besides, I had a very strong sense that I was to leave this battle with God.

It was hard to leave the station, but a week after I left, a group called Twin City Christian Television approached me about leading an effort to acquire an independent station which I would then own part of and manage. So God provided a job in my field—and I continue to speak and teach the gospel.

To this day, I'm mystified as to why my Christianity was ever a matter of such controversy and why my career was derailed because of my faith. I don't pretend to understand why it happened. But what I do know is that my faith was put to the test. I was forced to decide what was truly more important to me—a job I enjoyed or the freedom to express my faith. For me, in the end, there was no contest.

Life after the Flood

ANN CLELAND
as told to CAMERIN J. COURTNEY

*C*hristian faith is a grand
cathedral, with divinely
pictured windows. Standing
without, you see no glory, nor
can imagine any. But standing
within, every ray of light
reveals a harmony of
unspeakable splendors.

Nathaniel Hawthorne

A s I sat on my sister's dock watching the Fourth of July fireworks melt into the dusk, I felt God's peace. I had just completed three thousand dollars' worth of renovations to my beauty salon, and my fourteen-year-old daughter, Allison, and I had just emptied the last box into the home we'd moved into the week before. After three years of recovering from a painful divorce, I finally felt good about my life.

But on the fifth of July, it started to rain. And on the sixth it continued. And seventh. And eighth. City officials warned us that the swollen Mississippi was spilling into the nearby Raccoon River, threatening the residents of Des Moines. Day after day, I arrived at my salon to find yet another neighboring merchant had packed up and moved out. But I was worried about being able to pay my bills, so I stayed on.

About eight-thirty the morning of the tenth, Susan, a client of mine, called and said, "Ann, I'm coming over. You're evacuating." So Susan and another client, Rhonda—along with my receptionist and the woman who sells me hair products—packed up my salon as I finished up with the last few clients. By afternoon, we were wading through water to get from the salon to their trucks. I silently thanked God that these persistent women had prompted me to leave when I did. When we finished at the salon, I realized I was only half done. Less than a mile away, the flood waters also threatened my home.

By three-thirty in the afternoon, I was running frantically around my house. There were so many quick decisions to make. What did I want to keep? What could I leave behind? We were able to store most of my furniture in the attic, but we didn't have time for the kitchen appliances. Thank God Allison had gone to visit her father in Virginia.

That evening, I drove the wrong way down a one-way street—the only one still navigable—to a friend's house a few miles away. Through the downpour I could hardly see the frantic families scrambling to pack up their possessions and escape from the unrelenting waters. I was too exhausted to realize I had just been stripped of my source of income and my home.

For the next two weeks, I stayed with friends—a couple days here, a couple days there. I called Allison and told her I'd saved the cat and her bed—and she cried.

Until the waters receded, city authorities wouldn't allow us into our businesses or homes. I glued myself to the TV, but I could never identify my house or salon as the cameras panned over the flooded areas. I had no idea how much damage was being done. All I could do was pray for the best and prepare for the worst.

Finally, a week after the flood, we were allowed back into our soggy neighborhoods. The sight of my house brought tears of relief and frustration. A gray horizontal line—the filthy residue of flood waters—stretched across the front of my home about five feet above ground. When I opened the basement door and looked down, eight feet of river swirled at my toes. I opened my dishwasher and water poured out. The garage was carpeted with two inches of mud and snakes—and smelled like a sewer. Because the city's water plant had been flooded, we had no running water, so I collected rain from the eaves in a cooler and started scrubbing. At that point, I still thought I could live there—but I later realized that the twenty thousand dollars in needed repairs was more than I could afford. So I lost my three-thousand-dollar down payment—and my dream of owning a home for my daughter and me.

My beauty salon wasn't in much better condition. The work stations were mildewed and crumbled, and the reception desk disintegrated when we tried to move it. I also lost a hydraulic chair that had cost about a thousand dollars. Friends and volunteers gutted my salon while my two stylists and I continued to cut hair at a local salon that was gracious enough to house us for a few weeks. We joined the laborers every evening and worked until exhaustion took over.

But months of cutting hair all day and rebuilding my salon all evening brought on extreme fatigue. Allison took our flood losses pretty hard and had to work through serious grief and depression. I was forced to take out loans in order to rebuild my shop—and an eighty-seven thousand balloon payment came due in September.

Yet the generosity of friends and strangers poured into my life as quickly and unexpectedly as the flood waters. Volunteers from my church hauled the black, mucky carpet out of my house and washed off my flood-covered dishes. Workers from the Christian Relief Effort, a coalition of local churches, cleared out my rotting home. Donations flooded in. My church gave me $5,000. A Kiwanis group in Connecticut sent me $500. A friend in Iowa City sent me $165—money she and her beauty salon clients had raised for me. But my favorite memory of God's provision occurred one day while I was sobbing in the middle of my ruined salon, mourning over all I'd lost. A few volunteers stopped in with a check for $40 from a woman who was physically unable to help with sandbagging or construction. The money was earmarked for the first person they saw cry.

Within two weeks of the flood, the mom of my daughter's best friend helped us find an apartment, where we currently live. A man from church offered to redesign my salon at a fraction of what it should have cost me, and a local lumber store donated all of the doors, doorknobs, nails, and other hardware. Two volunteers appeared from nowhere to overhaul my ruined plumbing and electrical system. Piece by piece, we put my salon back together, relocating it in a much larger area that I had previously used for storage in the back of the building, allowing me to sublease the prime space in front. By September, I was back in business.

Some nights—when my requests for government assistance were denied, when a second flood threatened, when I didn't know where I'd be staying the next night—I would lie awake thinking about Noah adrift in the flood waters all those months. I wondered if he had felt as helpless, lonely, and afraid as I did. But month after month of God's compassionate provision changed my fear to renewed faith.

I now have a stained-glass window in the front of my renovated salon—a dove with an olive branch—as a constant reminder of the dry land God provides after the flood.

My Husband Forgave
My Unfaithfulness

KATHLEEN MALLOY*
as told to HOLLY G. MILLER

*The names in the article, including that of the author, have been changed for privacy.

*O*ften the difference between
a healthy marriage and a
defective one is not the
number or severity of
problems encountered but the
way problems are dealt with.

R. C. Sproul

When I admitted to my husband, Bob, that I had been unfaithful to him, I was prepared for every response except forgiveness.

For weeks I agonized about telling him the truth. The affair—a terrible, terrible mistake—was *over;* why did he need to know? Keeping it a secret was best, I decided, but I wondered if my motivation was to spare Bob the pain or to spare me the shame.

In the end, I had no choice: My emotions were a jumble of contradictions and wouldn't stay under wraps. Bob no longer believed me when I blamed my mood swings on PMS or my inability to return his hugs on my preoccupation with work. He wanted to know what was wrong, and I had run out of lies.

At age forty-one, I was an unlikely candidate for an extramarital affair. Bob and I had been married for nineteen years and were active in our church. I had just taken a job as a secretary in a large public-relations firm in the hope of boosting our kids' college fund.

Most of my friends already had found their way back to the careers they had put on hold when they married. For a long time I had envied their shop talk, expanding responsibilities, updated wardrobes, and the occasional splurges their salaries allowed. *Now it's my turn,* I thought.

Three days into my new job, I had my doubts. My skills were rusty, my confidence level nonexistent. After a couple of minutes in front of a computer screen, I wanted to wave a white flag and retreat home.

My supervisor quickly assigned Steve, the resident technology whiz, to bail me out. His duties included training new employees on the office information system, and he later joked that I was his greatest challenge. He recognized my insecurity and said all the right words of encouragement. He teased me just enough to help me relax, then proposed a crash course in data retrieval—whatever *that* was.

"Translation: Long hours and hard work," he cautioned. "But if you're willing, I'm willing."

He also was willing to schedule a couple of Saturday-morning sessions and reward my progress with follow-up lunches. He sent me funny messages via electronic mail and insisted I respond so I could learn the right codes and commands. I eagerly participated in this silent dialogue and didn't stop several weeks later when his notes took on a decidedly personal tone.

He seemed to notice everything about me—my revamped hairstyle, the new blazer, a different cologne—and wasted no time in complimenting me. Although his attention set off internal warning signals, I ignored them. I was an adult, after all. I could halt our friendship any time it became uncomfortable. For now, I was flattered.

On the surface, my marriage seemed strong enough to withstand any threats posed by a flirtatious computer trainer. For years Bob and I had enjoyed a warm, comfortable relationship, short on spontaneity but long on commitment. Our marriage was a well-tuned partnership: We knew our roles and went about them without a lot of communication. I loved Bob and he loved me, and daily assurances came not in words but in our willingness to pitch in and share duties.

If romance had slipped away, I never thought about its absence until it suddenly reappeared—courtesy of Steve—in the form of silly cards propped against my coffee mug, flowers tucked under my windshield wipers, and Post-it notes tacked to my computer screen. I was being pursued—and it felt good.

I found myself comparing Bob to Steve and always giving Steve the edge. Bob was dependable, Steve was exciting; Bob made me feel secure, Steve made me feel young; Bob wanted to build a future, Steve wanted to enjoy the present.

I couldn't talk to anyone about my confusion because then I'd have to justify my growing attachment to a man who wasn't my husband. I gradually withdrew from my family, our church, and our friends. They only reminded me that what I was doing was dangerous and wrong.

My new job with its long hours provided the perfect excuse for my spotty attendance at Wednesday night Bible study and for my decision to drop out of our church's couples club. Bob and our daughters never questioned my need to spend evenings in the den with stacks of papers from the office.

My involvement with Steve progressed from professional to emotional to sexual. I hated my double life and the lies I told to support it. Three months later, when my guilt became unbearable, I requested a transfer to a suburban office, a move that put Steve physically, if not emotionally, out of my life. I missed him, but I didn't miss the deception that was the foundation of the relationship. He accepted my decision with little argument, causing me to believe our affair had meant much more to me than to him. Distance brought clarity—and with it, more guilt. I tried to pretend the involvement had never happened. But it *had* happened, and my conscience wouldn't let me forget. I tried to get back in touch with my family and church, but those contacts made my secret more unbearable.

Why can't I put this behind me? I wondered. I hadn't been caught, no one was spreading gossip about me, and no one was challenging me to defend my actions. I still enjoyed a blemish-free reputation, and I was even being held up as a role model—the working wife and mom who successfully juggled career and family. But every time a friend said, "I wish I were more like you," I wanted to scream. I didn't deserve admiration.

My need to confess eventually caused me to tell Bob the truth. He had suspected something was wrong because I had struggled with bouts of the blues for weeks. I felt emotionally numb and had difficulty responding to his need for intimacy.

His love and trust were daily reminders of my unworthiness. I had to pay for my actions, and since he was the victim, I wanted him to deal me a harsh punishment. Still, I dreaded the confrontation and imagined the range of his reactions: First there would be disbelief, then hurt, then finally, anger.

What I never considered was the response that came after the tears, after the angry questions, after the talk of separation and divorce, and after our decision to try to restore our badly fractured marriage.

"First, we have to forgive," said Bob. We weren't sure we could do it; we only knew that with God's help, we wanted to try. And as hard as that would be for him, it would be even harder for me to forgive myself.

Healing came slowly. More than a year passed before I had sufficiently forgiven myself so I could accept God's grace. Up to that point, my faith seemed to increase my guilt instead of ease it. Familiar Scripture verses about fidelity and commitment jumped off the pages of my Bible and haunted instead of helped me. They reminded me that as a Christian I had known the difference between right and wrong, yet I had sinned anyway. Ignorance was no excuse for my actions. The burden of being a believer had never seemed heavier.

Our marriage was fragile, so Bob and I looked for ways to strengthen it. We tried too hard to make up for our mistakes. I overcompensated by acting the part of the perfect wife and mother, fussing with meals, keeping a spotless house, and doting on our daughters. Bob struggled to be more demonstrative by bringing me flowers and calling me from work just to say hello. Privately, I wondered if he was checking to see if I was at home when I said I would be. Could he ever trust me again?

We read a "how-to" book about revitalizing relationships and laughed at our clumsiness in carrying out its advice. The laughter did more good than the advice, and we decided there was a lesson in that, too. We needed to laugh and talk more.

We attended a marriage-enrichment seminar and picked through the platitudes for something that might ease the hurt. We visited a Christian counselor who helped us understand that "comfortable" marriages aren't always healthy ones. Prayer together became an essential part of our daily life and recovery.

Now, two years after my affair, our life is coming together. Although I still don't fully understand what caused me to do what I did, I pray that I've learned something from it. I know now that Christians, like everyone else, are vulnerable to temptation. And I understand that a marriage, even a good one, requires constant nurturing to sustain it.

Our relationship will never be the same because we will never be the same. Trust and respect have eroded, but perhaps in time they will be replenished. The fact that my unfaithfulness didn't become common knowledge now seems like a gift from God. He gave me a second chance, and this time, I pray I will use it wisely.

I Couldn't Love
My Mother

GLORIA CHISHOLM

The more we look at Scripture, the more convinced we are that love is something you do and something you don't do, whether you feel like it or not. Feeling like it just makes things easier.

Jill and Stuart Briscoe

Y our mother is dying of ovarian cancer," the doctor harshly pronounced. "The cancer cells on her ovaries are as numerous as snowflakes on a mountain." This strong, invincible woman who had given me birth was dying—and I felt nothing.

I guess somewhere along the line, I had quit trying to love my mother. Years and years of unresolved hurts had piled up in my heart, and I had decided she wasn't going to hurt me anymore—because if you don't love, you don't get hurt. Now I realized not only did I not feel *love* for her but I felt neutral. Numb.

These thoughts tormented me as I sat in the circle of women I prayed with weekly. I wanted to ask for prayer for my mother, but I didn't know what I wanted them to pray. The obvious maybe, a miracle healing? Salvation? Of course. And maybe God's comfort—that's the least I could have them pray for.

It was my turn. They were all staring at me. Maybe I should just pass. I didn't want them questioning me about our relationship. "I-I need prayer for my mother," I blurted out. "She-she's dying of cancer."

"What would you like us to pray?" one woman asked.

I knew it. Why did they have to ask that? Couldn't they just pray as the Holy Spirit led them?

"I-I want you to pray that she'll feel my love before she dies,"

I found myself blubbering. All of a sudden the thought of my mother facing death alone and feeling unloved by her only daughter filled me with unbearable grief. Still, I was asking God to do the impossible. How could she ever feel my love if I didn't love her? I sobbed.

I'd known for more than a year that my mother had cancer. But I just assumed the chemotherapy was taking care of it. Besides, I hardly ever saw her. I'd moved to a neighboring state six years before, and what little relationship we had at the time ceased altogether. We didn't even speak for a few years. When we did finally break the stony silence, it was still tense and superficial. For my kids' sake, I was grateful we were talking at all.

I'm not sure when the breakdown of our relationship first started. As a child, I must have involuntarily built a wall of protection around me that my mother never tried to break down. She was a hard-hearted woman who never seemed to love the little girl she had given birth to, and I couldn't remember her ever expressing love, care, or nurture of any kind. Mostly I felt abandoned by my mother, invisible.

I remember feeling hatred for her during my teen years. Then I became a Christian. I thought I'd forgiven her. All my zealous preaching to her about God surely proved that I cared for her soul. But I only succeeded in driving her further away by screaming, "You're going to hell if you don't repent," or "Mom, you're just a religious person—it doesn't really mean anything."

Of course, I was sorry for my harsh judgments now, but I had never told her. We didn't talk about things like that. We didn't talk about anything that mattered. My hurt ran so deep, I wasn't about to risk rejection by making the first move and putting my heart on the line.

A few days after I asked the women to pray, I went to visit my mother in the hospital. I wasn't prepared for the small, frail, bald woman who stared at me through sunken eyes, who tried to smile but whose every breath was laborious.

"You came," she said in an awed tone. "How are the kids? How's your job?" Every word took great effort. We made small talk.

Then, like a small earthquake, something began to rumble way down deep inside my heart. It suddenly occurred to me: My mother had been a single parent all of those years, just as I was now. She'd done the best she could on limited finances, energy, internal resources. No one understood that better than I. *Forgiveness, grace, mercy*—words that until now I had known only as cold concepts—suddenly became a reality as I felt them move through me from God to the one who had brought me life. I could actually feel the hatred go. Feelings of love, buried since childhood, now charged to the surface— and like an earthquake cracks the earth's surface, the hard outer shell of my heart began to crack.

"Mom, I love you." The words tore from my soul before I could stop them, exposing the feelings I'd carefully suppressed all those years.

Oh no, what had I done? I had uncovered all my buried feelings in one terrifying moment, and now they were out there, hanging in the thick air between us. I couldn't grab them back. I don't remember a time when I felt more vulnerable. I had foolishly set myself up to be abandoned again. But that was the risk. . . .

Then she spoke slowly, carefully, the words I'd longed to hear all of my life: "I love you, too." She paused, then took a deep breath. "You know, every morning for the last few years, I wake up, and the first thought on my mind is 'I don't have a daughter anymore.'"

What? She cared? She actually cared whether she had a daughter or not? Was I really hearing this? But the pain in her eyes spoke even louder than her words.

For three hours we talked. No, not rehashing every rotten thing we'd said or done to each other (although I did ask her to forgive me for how blunt I was as a new Christian). We simply talked about the kinds of stuff mothers and daughters talk about. And we loved each other.

"Why did this have to come so late?" she asked as I finally got ready to leave.

I shook my head. "I don't know." But to myself I thought, *It's never too late to love.*

And then she spoke longingly, "I wish I could feel God the way you do."

"Mom, you can." *Right now,* I thought. The miracle of my love expressed was God's precious gift to my mother this day. I prayed she wouldn't fail to recognize it.

I never saw her again. Three weeks later she was gone. But during those three weeks we talked on the phone many times—long-distance conversations, but a closer connection than ever before. And we weren't the only ones connecting. "I've prayed to God more in these last few weeks than in my whole life," she told me.

Was my risk of abandonment worth it? Is there anyone anywhere who would trade three weeks of precious love between mother and daughter for a lifetime of numbness and walled-off feelings?

Not me. And I take more risks now. I make it a point to charge through my own kids' self-protective barriers each day with a sandwich, a hug, a genuine "I'm sorry" when I've hurt someone—to show them God's faithful kind of love.

Thanks, Mom. Knowing you—even if only for three weeks—has changed my life.

Someone has to jump first. This time it happened to be me. I will be forever grateful I did.

The Day the
Hurricane Hit

CHRISTINE MILES

The Lord doesn't promise to
give us something to take so
we can handle our weary
moments. He promises us
himself. That is all. And that
is enough.

Charles R. Swindoll

It was the third weekend of August, and our family had just returned home from vacation. Amid unpacking and doing laundry, I wasn't focused on the news. But late Saturday night, our older daughter, Jennifer, fourteen, informed me that her friends' parents were stocking up on hurricane supplies. We quickly turned on the weather channel, and there it was: Hurricane Andrew—headed straight for Miami!

Jenny and I hurried to the grocery store, but we were too late. Supplies of water, candles, and batteries were sold out. As we stood in line for three hours to buy juice, soft drinks, cookies, and canned goods, we joked with the other women in line about being stuck in the candy aisle and having our willpower give out.

But when Sunday morning, August 23, dawned, it was time to get serious. I washed and disinfected containers for drinking water and rounded up our supplies. My husband, Art, spent the day putting up hurricane shutters—heavy corrugated metal to block out dangerous winds. The full force of the storm was expected to hit sometime after midnight, so I prepared a "safe room"—our downstairs bathroom. In it were mattresses, a transistor radio, first-aid supplies, and water. In my mounting hysteria, I even insisted we include four life jackets. I pictured our house blowing away and my family unconscious in flooded streets.

My husband slept peacefully that evening, but twelve-year-old Kim, Jenny, and I stayed up reading Psalms and picking out verses that reminded us of God's control. We read Psalm 29, a stormy psalm, which reassured us that God speaks in the thunder and the lightning.

The girls and I finally catnapped on a sofa bed, protecting ourselves from the possibility of shattered glass from the sliding glass door by placing an upright mattress against it. But by early morning, when our electricity failed and objects started slamming against our hurricane shutters, we knew it was time to retreat to our safe room. All four of us—plus our dog—squeezed into the bathroom.

As the winds increased, the house buckled and shuddered. Our ears popped from the pressure. Water poured in, seeping onto the mattresses. Art and I fought against the wind, bracing ourselves against the bathroom door. On the radio, hysterical callers to the station were crying, afraid they were going to die. Outside, the high-pitched, furious winds and rain constantly battered our house and bounced off the shutters. *Our entire house is going to collapse,* I thought, panic-stricken—but I tried to hide my fear from our girls.

To distract ourselves from the storm's ferocity, we sang Scripture songs. After what seemed like an eternity, we stopped having to strain against the bathroom door to keep it closed. Our ears stopped hurting. The eye of the storm had passed over us.

When Art and I cautiously emerged from the bathroom to survey the damage, we saw the shutters were still secure. Then why was our first floor flooding?

Art and Jenny went upstairs. To their shock, they discovered Jenny's bedroom had lost a large portion of roof. We didn't have much time before the second half of the storm passed over us. Would we be safe if we stayed in our house—or should we find shelter elsewhere? To our surprise, our telephone still worked. We called our neighbors, the Mahoneys, and thankfully they answered. "Do you still have a roof?" we asked.

"Yes," they replied. "Come on over!"

Art and I gently opened our front door. The force of the wind almost blew us away. Tree branches and other objects swirled crazily around. How would we get to our neighbors?

Then we saw it—a most beautiful sight: our neighbor's brother-in-law, dressed in a full-length yellow slicker and bicycle helmet, carrying a searchlight. One by one, Jenny, Kim, Art, and I ran outside toward him as he helped us fight the wind and run into their house.

We spent the rest of the storm with the Mahoneys in their family room, huddled in a closet or under pillows. After several hours, the winds subsided. Hurricane Andrew had run its course.

Everyone ventured outside to survey the destruction. Not a single house in our neighborhood remained undamaged! Many houses had been completely destroyed. We stumbled from house to house, asking, "Is everyone all right?" It was a miracle no one in our subdivision was killed. Although Hurricane Andrew was over, what we thought was the end was really just the beginning.

The next day, August 25, was our twenty-second wedding anniversary. As Art and I went back to our home to clean out debris and salvage what we could, he handed me an anniversary card that somehow he had saved. I fell apart, crying, because I didn't have one for him. He just smiled and said, "Don't worry. This is one anniversary I'll never forget."

Later that day, an acquaintance who is a roofer sent two men over to patch our roof, but they had no materials. We scoured the green belt behind the house and found part of our roof, which we used along with our bed boards as a temporary patch.

With no roof over our heads, we—along with two other families—moved in with the Mahoneys. For a week we worked on our houses without water or power, bathing in the briny lake water behind our house, drinking the water we had stored before Hurricane Andrew roared through our lives. Military helicopters flew overhead constantly. Our primitive living conditions—combined with the overt military presence—were disorienting. We felt as though we were living in a war zone. In the Florida heat and humidity, the stench of mildew was nauseating. The enormity of the devastation surrounding us physically and emotionally overwhelmed us.

It took months to rebuild our house. Our walls were crumbling, and mildew grew everywhere. We even had mushrooms sprouting in our living room! Carpets needed to be ripped up and tile torn out. Cabinetry warped and buckled, fixtures rusted. Even though my parents came down from Canada to help us in the rebuilding process, life in a construction zone—stumbling over people and boxes, scheduling contractors for repairs, and never knowing whether something had been salvaged or lost in the storm—was extremely stressful.

For the first month especially, because of hazardous travel, limited supplies, and unavailable services, everything was a major problem. Kim tripped over a generator cord at church and broke her foot. Our dog almost died. Jenny lost all of her furniture, and Kim lost most of her clothes, stuffed animals, and other mementos. What I missed most was my sense of security. I had lost my place to "be."

Despite the stress and discouragement of the last several months, God has been faithful. We expected our church family to be concerned, and they were. What we didn't expect were the many kindnesses from others. Kim's former science teacher gave us battery-powered candles and other supplies. Jenny's former Girl Scout leader arrived with huge bags of ice. And our neighbor's future niece-in-law did a load of laundry for us. Many people showed us God's love and concern.

The Lord even showed us his sense of humor in the midst of this catastrophe. One day, while everyone worked on roof repairs in ninety-degree temperatures, a neighborhood boy arrived with a wheelbarrow full of ice cream that had been given away by the local supermarket because its freezer was failing. We had a feast!

It's been eleven months since Hurricane Andrew hit, and I'm still tired. I suspect my fatigue has emotional *and* spiritual components. Even though our house is finally back together, I don't always realize something's missing until I need it. Sometimes I feel as though we'll never lead a normal life again.

But our family's learned that in a crisis, material things don't matter. Family, friends, faith in the Lord—these are the things that count. We've been blessed by becoming involved in hurricane-relief efforts—helping those whose losses were much greater than ours. Although I've struggled less with losing individual items than with losing my sense of security, I remind myself how I have a home in heaven that Jesus is already preparing just for me—and I won't even have to schedule contractors for it!

This summer, when hurricanes form, I think I'll be afraid. But I know God's in control and that I can cling to the solid Rock, the Rock of my salvation. I'll always remember Psalm 46:1 "God is our refuge and strength, an ever-present help in trouble." He proved that to me through Hurricane Andrew.

I Was a Prisoner of Panic Attacks

Marian V. Liautaud

The wise man in the storm
prays to God, not for safety
from danger, but for
deliverance from fear. It is the
storm within which endangers
him. Not the storm without.

Ralph Waldo Emerson

After the birth of our first son, I decided to explore some new employment options. While I knew the increased responsibilities of parenting and working to make financial ends meet would gradually take their toll, I felt confident I could handle them.

However one day, while interviewing with my prospective employer, something terrifying happened. The windowless room where the interview took place closed in around me, the air became thin, my throat tightened, and the rushing in my head became deafening. All I could think was *I've got to get out.*

My mind and heart raced for what seemed an eternity as I feigned composure. Somehow, I made it through the meeting without giving my interviewer a clue that I had been seconds away from fleeing his office or passing out on the spot.

What I didn't know then was that I had experienced a panic attack, a common but little-talked-about reaction to stress many women suffer from. My fear of experiencing another attack set in motion a vicious cycle of recurring episodes.

No one, except my husband, Dan, knew I suffered from extreme anxiety. He listened compassionately to my daily reports of exhausting attacks, but neither of us understood their cause. I feared being viewed as unstable, so instead of seeking professional help, I withdrew into my own private world of terror. For ten to twenty minutes several times a day, usually during meetings, I endured a rush of the fight-or-flight instinct one usually experiences in life-threatening situations. Anxiety eventually trickled into every area of my life. It hit its peak one evening when I drove home alone from a trade show I had attended in the city. I felt boxed in by the other cars on the highway. My head started to spin, and my eyes had difficulty focusing in the twilight. I knew I needed help. After that night, even common, nonthreatening situations paralyzed me.

I went to my doctor for a complete physical. When I told him my symptoms, I was sure he would say I was on the verge of a breakdown or suffering from some rare blood disease. Instead, he simply prescribed a mild depressant to help me cope physically with stress.

I left his office even more despondent than when I had gone in. *Here I am, with a faith that is supposed to empower me,* I thought. *Depressants are for people who can't cope. Why can't I overcome these attacks through prayer?* So I refused to fill my prescription and subconsciously waited for God to bail me out. For the next year and a half, I hoped for a miracle and struggled on my own.

Prayer became an integral part of my anxiety-control regimen and helped me to cope temporarily. In the midst of a panic attack, I imagined every breath I took was filled with the Spirit. I mentally repeated *I am with you* until my feelings of fear subsided.

Prayer also led to other discoveries about myself and my lifestyle. I realized that when I first started having panic attacks, Dan and I had been married just over a year, we had bought our first home, had a baby, and both worked full-time jobs on opposite shifts. Little wonder I was burning out.

Gradually, I felt God's prompting to make some deliberate

changes in my life. I left my former job when our second son was born and began working part time at a new office two months later. Because I worked fewer hours and the stress level was much lower, I figured panic attacks were a thing of the past. But fear gradually crept back into my life.

Meetings again became cause for sheer terror. I found it difficult to contribute to group discussions and withdrew into fearful silence. *Lord,* I begged, *why is this happening again? Why am I unable to handle stress like everyone else?*

After living three years with panic dominating my life, I was in no mood to tough it out on my own this time. I finally sought counseling.

In three visits my psychologist helped me understand how panic attacks happen. Because of unconscious breathing changes—from slow and steady to shallow and rapid—the brain perceives danger and sends out a dose of adrenaline to assist in an escape—which is of little use when you are immobilized in a chair during a business meeting.

What I do now to counter these faulty survival mechanisms is to say internally, *I am safe, God is with me, Christ is in me, I am safe,* until my mind and body really believe it. I imagine a place where I feel safe—like a room in my home—to further convince my mind I'm free from harm. And I concentrate on slow, deep breathing until I've regained composure.

I have finally come to understand that panic attacks are not an indication of a weak faith. They are a physical and emotional response to stress. Where faith becomes part of the picture, though, is in my response to the attacks. Rather than let fear rule my life, I use it as a barometer. Often I discover that when the pressure is high, my relationships to Christ, family, and work are skewed. Some of the clearest signs God gives me to get back on track are the growing symptoms of stress I experience.

Panic attacks are exhausting to live with. And often I wonder why I seem predisposed to having them. But I have always felt God's strength holding me up and giving me comfort. Somehow, I can't help but think that if the net effect of my panic attacks has served to draw me closer to him, then perhaps this is one affliction worth living with.

Please, God, Not Alzheimer's

RUTH CRAWFORD LINDSEY

*We are not necessarily
doubting that God will do the
best for us, we are wondering
how painful the best will turn
out to be.*

C. S. Lewis

W hen the neurologist told me my husband, Jack, had Alzheimer's disease, I felt as though the air was sucked from the room. *Oh, God, no,* my heart pounded. *Please, not that.*

The diagnosis came within six months of Jack's having almost died with Rocky Mountain spotted fever the previous summer. His recovery had been slow, and although his doctors had assured me he was "as good as new," his personality had changed. He didn't want me out of his sight; he kept asking the same questions over and over; he became careless with his appearance and had to be urged even to take a bath.

Even before Jack's bout with spotted fever, he'd been having trouble following instructions at work. A professional printer with more than twenty-five years of experience at layout, he could no longer handle the stressful deadlines. Twice his foreman had reassigned him to easier jobs. Finding his time card was a daily challenge. Sometimes he punched someone else's card, much to that employee's consternation.

Jack was fifty-five; I was seven years younger. We had been married for only five years. After having served thirteen years as a single missionary-teacher in Brazil, I had thought I would remain unmarried the rest of my life. Then I met Jack, who fell in love with me at first sight, he said. After we married, I soon concluded that being single had been OK—but being happily married was much better. Now Jack's diagnosis shattered my dreams of having a lifelong companion with whom I could share my life.

Along with others, I prayed earnestly for Jack's healing. Repeatedly I quoted Genesis 18:14: "Is anything too hard for the Lord?" I recited Psalm 103:2-3: "Praise the Lord, O my soul, . . . who . . . heals all your diseases." I reviewed the many instances of healing in Jesus' earthly ministry and reminded myself that "Jesus Christ is the same yesterday and today and forever" (Heb. 13:8). When I finally became quiet before the Lord, listening instead of talking, he spoke to my spirit: *I have not forsaken you. Don't be afraid. Trust me. My grace will always be greater than your need.*

Like persistent termites, the disease silently devoured Jack's short-term memory, coordination, and judgment and left just a shell with an outward appearance of health.

I never knew what to expect. One summer Jack manually caught and squashed thousands of Japanese beetles between his thumb and forefinger. Once he cross-connected the booster cables while attempting to jump-start the neighbor's car. He became my shadow, not allowing me even five minutes of privacy in the bathroom.

When I began attending meetings of an Alzheimer's support group, I learned that bizarre behavior ordinarily accompanies that disease. My participation in the meetings was minimal at first. I hesitated to publicize what was happening at our house. Soon, however, I learned that talking about it was therapeutic. People in the group were at different stages in the journey. Some were caring for family members at home; others had been forced to place their loved ones in a nursing home already. I silently prayed I could continue taking care of Jack at home.

About five years after the diagnosis, changes in Jack's condition accelerated. He became agitated and angry for no apparent cause. I could not reason with him. He accused me of infidelity and threatened revenge. Although I knew in my heart this wasn't the "real Jack," his words hurt. I cried, but my crying just made matters worse.

The nights were worse than the days. Because he couldn't sleep, neither did I. He paced constantly. Sometimes he left the house scantily clothed; once he exited naked.

Soon he required around-the-clock care. When I admitted him to a nursing home one Friday afternoon, my heart broke. He didn't understand why we had to be separated.

The first visits were extremely difficult for me. Somehow I would manage to hold myself together until I left the premises—then sobs would wrench my body.

Surprisingly, Jack adjusted quickly to the nursing-home routine. Within a few weeks he seemed not to have remembered ever living anywhere else. He would watch for me and clap his hands when he saw me arriving. We strolled on the premises and played "catch" with a purple fuzzy Koosh ball designed for preschoolers.

My stepchildren found it emotionally draining to visit Jack in the nursing home. Their visits became less frequent. Then one day he no longer recognized them at all. After that, they virtually stopped going.

There were other evidences, too, of declension. For example, he forgot how to tie his shoes. Later he couldn't tell which shoe went on which foot. He became incapable of shaving, bathing, and brushing his teeth. Eventually he became incontinent. For the past three years he has been totally dependent on others, even for spoon-feeding.

We had always expressed our love to each other. Daily at the nursing home I continued to assure him of my love. My heart

was warmed when he would respond with "I love you, too."
With time, that got shortened to a faltering "I . . . love . . . you,"
then to "I . . . love . . . ," and finally to "I . . . I . . . I. . . ." Then
followed weeks of silence.

"Lord," I prayed, "are my words getting through? Please give
me the assurance that Jack feels loved."

Though he didn't respond, I kept talking to Jack, hoping my
words were penetrating his tangled brain cells. Then one day
in 1993, when I again said, "I love you, Jack," he replied slowly
but clearly, "I . . . know . . . that."

He has not spoken a word since. I'm confident, however,
that he still understands some, at least, of what I tell him. He
responds to my voice and touch. Whether he still compre-
hends that I'm his wife, I don't know.

Jack's condition has remained relatively stable for the past
year. I teach full time at a local college, but my class schedule
permits me to spend a couple of hours with him at noon each
day. The nursing home is understaffed, so I do whatever I can
to make Jack more comfortable—shaving him, cleaning his
teeth, or even changing soiled underclothes. Then I feed him.
Finally, I walk with him, slowing my pace to his four-inch-step
shuffle, while talking to him, quoting Scripture, or softly
singing choruses and hymns he himself sang in bygone years.

Several years ago, I concluded Jack would not benefit from
sadness or pity. I noticed, in fact, that he reacted to the moods
of people around him. I determined to learn to laugh again
and to try to bring laughter back into his life.

I was amused the first time I saw him talking with his
almost toothless, grinning reflection in the mirror while I
cleaned his dentures. He pointed and jabbered, only to be
pointed back at and jabbered to. I've seen each of them
laughingly try to hand the other a glass of water.

One rainy day we were tossing the Koosh ball back and

forth in his room. He pitched it so one of the rubbery fibers caught on a rough place in the ceiling. There the ball hung, dangling over our heads. He began to laugh, and I joined him. The laughter was contagious. Within minutes several residents and nursing assistants were at his door to see what was funny. They, too, laughed.

When I leave the nursing home, I consciously relinquish Jack to the staff's care. At home I keenly miss him and often think about how things might have been. Sometimes I dream he's by my side, only to awaken, reach for him, and touch an empty pillow.

Having observed that the caregiver sometimes becomes the second victim of Alzheimer's, often being left scarred for life, I have tried to avoid that fate. Instead of becoming a recluse, I have actually increased my efforts to cultivate a network of friends. I attend church regularly and sometimes go to concerts and other performances. Gardening being my favorite pastime, I spend many pleasant hours working in my backyard. Digging in the dirt and watching things grow are therapeutic for me. Too, the garden provides delicious fresh vegetables for home-cooked meals, to which I often invite friends. I'm learning to cope.

Caring and coping have brought some changes into my own life. Through caregiving, I've learned more about God's love. God loves me regardless of how I respond to his love—or even if I don't respond at all.

There is no glimmer of recognition or word of thanks when I do a "dirty job" to make Jack more comfortable. On the contrary, sometimes he becomes agitated and lashes out at me, grabbing my wrists and twisting them. Instead of retorting, "That does it! I'll not help you anymore," I excuse his behavior because he doesn't understand what he's doing. And

I've gone back the next day, perhaps with a wrist brace on, to continue to do whatever I can for him.

I can recall times when I've lashed out at God, when I've sulked, when I've neglected fellowshiping with him, when I didn't acknowledge his goodness. But that didn't drive God away. Much as I coax Jack, the Lord would say, *Come on. I'll help you. I love you.*

In addition, I'm learning God's grace is provided as I need it. Corrie ten Boom once questioned her father about dying grace, fearing she didn't have it. He reminded her that when she traveled by train as a child, he didn't give her the ticket until departure time. The same principle applies to grace. When we need it, it's there.

If twelve years ago I had been told I would do some of the things for Jack I have done and am doing, I would have said, "I can't do it." And at that time, I couldn't have. But then I didn't have to. When grace has been needed, however, grace has been provided—just as God promised.

The Most Terrifying Night of My Life

MARIE CLAUSEN

When I lose sight of trust, I become so preoccupied with protecting myself that I forget man can be redeemed. Even more tragic, I may close myself off from the very people who need God's glory the most. But God's plan is redemption, not safety.

Ruth Senter

S tatistics indicate one out of three women will be sexually assaulted in her lifetime," the television newscaster announced one fall afternoon.

While I listened attentively to the program, I never seriously considered the possibility of being raped. Surely God would protect me from such a despicable crime, I thought. Little did I know what my future held.

Later that same night, after I got into bed, I heard a strange noise in my apartment. Seconds later, my parakeet began thrashing around in his cage. I got out of bed to investigate, but before I could switch on a light, something swept through my bedroom door, hitting me like a speeding freight train. A stranger in dark clothes threw me back on my bed and wrapped his fingers around my throat, choking me until I could no longer scream or breathe.

The most terrifying night of my life had just begun.

As soon as I realized my assailant's intent, I cried out to Jesus for help, hoping the very utterance of his name would drive the man away. Certain I was going to be killed, I silently prayed—oh, how I prayed—for God's intervention, his protection, and his wisdom.

After nearly forty-five minutes, my assailant disappeared, leaving me handcuffed and gagged. *Oh Lord, is it over yet? Is he gone?* I wasn't sure, but I was too frightened to move. When he didn't return after ten minutes, I worked the gag out of my mouth, but my hands remained tightly handcuffed behind my back. Somehow I managed to dial 911 and summon help. Though it seemed like several hours, four minutes later the police arrived, finding me huddled naked beside my bed, sobbing uncontrollably.

"It's OK, Marie, it wasn't your fault," the hospital's rape crisis counselor said soothingly an hour or two later. But I couldn't stop crying. "Maybe I left my sliding door unlocked," I sobbed. "Marie, it doesn't matter what you may have done; he didn't have any right to come into your apartment. It wasn't your fault, Marie. Do you hear me? It *wasn't* your fault!" I knew she was right—but it still hurt.

The next several days were a blur. Safe in the home of dear friends, I began the long road to recovery by telling them all the sordid details of what had happened. It was like a poison inside of me that had to come out. I still wonder if they realize how much their compassion—their willingness to listen and cry with me—sped up the healing process.

Nine days after the rape, determined not to let my assailant ruin my life, I steeled myself to go back home. I knew running away wouldn't solve anything; I had to face my fear head-on. That first night was the hardest; I honestly didn't know if I could endure. But as the months passed, I began to relax.

I wish I could say that now, two years later, everything is back to normal. But I know my life has been changed forever. Strange sounds still paralyze me—especially at night—so a wireless security system, timers, and a locked bedroom door have become a way of life—at least for now.

But God has promised that all things will work together for good, so I'm finding constructive ways to channel my anger.

I'm learning to look for the good things that have emerged from that night.

One of the "good things" has been the opportunity to tell people what I've learned about rape, to help them understand that rape is *never* justifiable, no matter who the man is—a stranger, an acquaintance, a date, or even a mate. Rape is never about sex, passion, or manhood—it's about violence.

I also want them to know no woman should ever feel ashamed or guilty about being raped. Like any other victim, I did not deserve to be raped, so there is no reason to feel shame. What a miracle it is to be able to say that! Even more miraculous is realizing I'm not just a *victim* of rape or a *survivor.* I am a *victor!*

I'm a victor because I have learned how to go on living. It wasn't easy, and it took a lot of time and prayer. But I realized nothing could change what had happened, so I decided to focus on God's blessings and mercies instead: I wasn't physically hurt except for a few bruises; the police treated me with remarkable sensitivity and compassion; I learned how many wonderful, caring friends I have.

My faith is deeper—stronger—because of that night. God has shown me in countless ways how much he loves me. Whenever I'm about to forget his faithfulness, he reminds me of his promise in Jeremiah 29:11: " 'For I know the plans I have for you,' declares the Lord, 'plans to prosper you and not to harm you, plans to give you hope and a future.' " Whenever I think about the evil my assailant inflicted on me, I try to focus on the bigger picture—I remember Joseph's ability to look beyond the evil of his brothers, who sold him into slavery in Egypt. Instead of choosing bitterness, Joseph deliberately chose to see with eyes of faith God's blessings and the good accomplished through his circumstances.

I've learned firsthand that God understands our pain. He

feels it as intensely as we do, and he really is there to comfort us during those times. So it is with renewed conviction and faith that I continue to draw close—especially when the pain is too much to bear—until I come into his presence for eternity.

My Prayers Went Unanswered

HELEN GRACE LESCHEID

Those who are happiest are not necessarily those for whom life has been easiest. Emotional stability is an attitude. It is refusing to yield to depression and fear, even when black clouds float overhead. It is improving that which can be improved and accepting that which is inevitable.

James Dobson

When Bill, my husband of twenty-eight years, signed himself into a psychiatric hospital on a warm September day, our family of seven was devastated. After struggling under an onslaught of personal and professional pressures—including grief over the loss of both father and mother within six months—Bill had become severely depressed.

Our whole community, who knew Bill as a strong Christian leader and well-loved high school teacher, was in shock. Concerned Christian friends rallied around us and promised to pray. Messages of hope kept pouring in—and I welcomed each one.

"Your husband will be healed," some said with finality, as though God himself had spoken. Others gave me Scriptures of hope and comfort. Letters from three continents assured me that our family name came up repeatedly in prayer groups. Daily, earnest prayers, prayed in Jesus' name—some with tears and fasting—were offered on our behalf.

But over the months, despite the continual prayers, Bill's condition worsened. Every treatment failed. Varied drugs brought horrifying side effects. Counseling sessions plunged him into deeper despair.

Bill's depression became so severe that he attempted suicide four times and threatened to kill me and the children. He was transferred from our local hospital to the university hospital, then to the locked ward of the provincial mental hospital.

When our prayers for my husband's healing didn't achieve the desired results, some people offered me prayer formulas. "You must say these specific words," they suggested. Others asked if there were some sinful attitude that kept God from answering our prayers.

My friends' well-meant suggestions made me introspective. I searched my heart again and again and repented of every harsh word spoken, every unkind attitude expressed. When my own shortcomings loomed to despair-sized proportions, I clung to the words, "But you know that he [Christ] appeared so that he might take away our sins" (1 John 3:5).

I realized that God would hear my cries, not because of my righteousness or ability to pray correctly, but because of who he is—a faithful, loving God whose nature is to bless his children.

But many times what was happening to our family looked more like calamities than blessings—a car crash totaled my sturdy Volvo, a gasoline explosion sent our thirteen-year-old son to the hospital, a personal illness made me miss many days at work. These and other stresses bombarded us.

Meanwhile, my strong husband became so weak he had to be brought into the visiting lounge in a wheelchair. His face was badly bruised and stitched from a nasty fall. As I listened to my husband's confused ramblings, I'd still my pounding heart with, *My hope is not in psychiatry but in God—and he isn't finished yet.*

A short distance from our provincial mental hospital, a local church had mounted a sign beside the freeway: "Jesus is Lord." Every time I passed that sign, I pondered those words. Was Jesus master of every situation? Could I trust God even when so many things went wrong? Should we measure God's love by the good things he pours into our lives or by what the Bible says about him? I decided that since God's love is eternal, it had to be the same whether my personal experience was good or bad.

I encouraged our children to accompany me to the hospital and tell their dad about school and the other activities they were involved in. On warm days, we'd stroll across the landscaped hospital grounds. Once we went into the music room where our daughter played the piano and we sang some familiar hymns together. But most of the time, we just sat in the smoke-filled lounge with Bill.

In front of their dad, the children tried to be cheerful and brave. Then later, on our way home, I'd hear their brokenhearted sobs or confused anger. "Where is God in all this?" "Why doesn't he answer our prayers?"

Seeing our children suffer so deeply was like a knife boring into my heart. How could I comfort them when I, too, was hurting badly? My own emotional energy depleted, I'd pour out my frustration before the Lord. "I just don't know what to say anymore," I'd confess. "But you're the God of all comfort, aren't you? You comfort them now."

Although I wanted to remain honest with our children, I determined to speak words of hope, not despair, and keep life as normal as possible for them. I was enabled to do this by the kind people God brought into my life—people who didn't interpret my outpourings of pain as a lack of faith but affirmed me as a child of God in whom he was pleased.

One such friend was Kay. She reminded me of the story of Lazarus and his sisters, especially of Martha's heart-wrenching words after her brother had died: "Lord, . . . if you had been here, my brother would not have died. But I know that even now God will give you whatever you ask" (John 11:21-22).

"Even now, Helen," she whispered. "God is with you, and he knows what he's doing—*even now.*"

To give myself a daily visual reminder of this fact, I wrote on a card "I've decided God is good and he can be trusted *even now,*" and pinned it to a bulletin board beside our kitchen phone.

Following a series of electric shock treatments, my husband improved enough to be discharged from the hospital. We were elated and deeply grateful. I told our friends, "God has answered your many prayers. Our nightmare has ended. Now we can forget the whole thing and get on with our lives."

But about two weeks later, Bill didn't want to get out of bed. With sinking heart, I watched the horrible downward spiral again.

Bill was readmitted to the hospital. More electric treatments, more drugs with frightening side effects, more therapy. The hopes-raised-and-dashed cycle repeated again and again.

One day, several years into the depression, Bill's psychiatrist leveled with me. "It could take another twenty years for any significant change in your husband," he said. "Soon he will be moved to the long-term care unit with other patients resistant to treatment."

Stunned with grief, I went for a long walk on our country road. *What's the good of praying and believing?* I railed at God. *Everything is taking its natural course, just as though you don't exist!* As I walked along, I saw a neighbor maneuver his tractor across the field. In the past, I'd felt sorry for him—he didn't attend church anywhere. Now a wave of understanding washed over me: *I know why you don't believe in God.*

But is he better off than you? a quiet voice asked. *When problems crash into his life, where does he turn for comfort? To whom can he pour out his grief?*

Immediately, I saw my mistake: I'd been focusing on my

hopeless circumstances instead of on the God of hope. Despite the doctor's gloomy prognosis, had God changed? Wasn't he still the same loving God of the Bible I'd come to trust? How often in the past I'd been surprised by God's tender ways of letting me know his love for me: a good night's sleep, some unexpected kindness. Wouldn't God continue to care for me in this meaningful way—regardless of the outcome of my husband's illness?

"Oh God," I whispered, "of course you're still with me—even now—in this darkness." The comfort I felt then was as real as though I'd been physically hugged. My doubts vanished, and a deep quiet flooded my heart.

It was all right not to understand God's seeming lack of intervention. It was all right that in myself I didn't have the resources to cope. God loved me and wanted the best for me and our family. As long as this was true, our family would survive. We'd have to make some adjustments, but we'd cope. God would see to it that we had the necessary resources.

Surprisingly, soon after the psychiatrists had sounded the "no hope" for my husband, he began to make tiny signs of wanting to come back to us. He'd express pleasure in my visits and occasionally even call home on the telephone. He'd listen more attentively to what the children were telling him and ask some questions. He even expressed hope that one day he'd be feeling better. Eventually, he asked to be discharged from the hospital—he felt he needed to face the real world in order to get well.

So, on July 10, my husband came home to stay. But since he'd been institutionalized for four years, even going into a bank or grocery store would trigger an intense anxiety attack. As a result, during that first year, my husband was hospitalized seven times. Each time, God gave him the courage to come back out and the hope to try again.

I couldn't have survived that turbulent time of rehabilitation had it not been for God's abiding presence, my family and friends, and my part-time job. For every situation, God supplied what I needed to cope.

Eventually, my husband realized that sitting idle and brooding didn't help him; he needed a job. But teaching was out of the question, and who would hire a man in his fifties? So, he put an ad in our church bulletin: "Want your grass cut? Bill Lescheid will give you reliable service."

We had no idea that one of Bill's first lawn-cutting customers owned a construction company. But God knew. At the end of the summer, when my husband's seasonal job was about to end, this man offered him a part-time job at the construction sites. And when the construction industry suffered a slump, his present job surfaced—working as a laborer at a recreational vehicle center.

Now when people observe my husband's energetic days and ability to function well without any medication, they want to know, "What exactly happened to bring about the turn-around?"

"God did it," I say truthfully.

"But why didn't it happen sooner?"

I don't know. But one thing I do know for certain: God is good; he is sovereign; and he knows that loving plan mapped out for our lives and the perfect timing of all events.

Something's happened to me as I've interacted with God in persistent prayer. Little by little, the realization has grown that God is a good Father who does the right thing for each of his children. And I've found this wonderful fact to be as true in the dark as it is in the light.

My Messiah, Too

LESLIE SHAPIRO WRIGHT

The Cross is God's truth
about us, and therefore it is
the only power which can
make us truthful. When we
know the Cross, we are no
longer afraid of the truth.

Dietrich Bonhoeffer

I never want to see you again or hear about your God, Jesus!" I adamantly told my fiancé, Harry, as I stalked into my parents' house. "I believe in the God of Abraham, Isaac, and Jacob. I don't need *your* God!"

A Jewish girl believing in Jesus? Impossible! I was unwilling to confront the reality that Jesus was the promised Messiah of the Jewish people—and my Messiah as well.

Over the previous months, Harry and I had often discussed the claims of Jesus, but that night—as Harry once again presented his "case" for Jesus Christ—he read me a passage of Scripture that was obviously talking about Jesus. Objecting, I told him, "Harry, of course that passage of Scripture refers to Jesus—you're reading about him from the New Testament!" I had Harry this time!

But Harry surprised me by answering, "No, Leslie, I wasn't reading from the New Testament; I was reading from the Old."

I grabbed the Bible from him. Surely he was kidding me—but he wasn't! Reading Isaiah 53, I realized it described the Jesus I'd heard about at Harry's church. I put the Bible down. I could no longer deny it—Jesus Christ *was* the Messiah the prophets had spoken of.

Suddenly, it became too much for me. How could I turn my

back on everything I had known since childhood—my Jewish heritage and way of life? What would my family and friends say? I was Jewish—and Jews did *not* believe in Jesus!

I demanded that Harry take me home. I was sure I was finished hearing about Jesus—and just as sure that our engagement was over.

Harry left, and I went to bed—but all I did was toss and turn. I thought about my childhood, how my mother had lit the Sabbath candles at sundown every Friday night and the memorial (Yahrzeit) candles on the anniversary of the death of a loved one. Even though we were not strict adherents to the Jewish faith, my family held to some Jewish traditions.

I remembered the taunts hurled at me by classmates: "You Jews killed Jesus Christ!" I never understood their remarks then, because I had no idea who Jesus was—but I had begun to think of him as my enemy!

I thought back to high school, when I started to take an active interest in Judaism. I wanted to learn more about my heritage, so I began attending the synagogue every Friday night. I learned the Hebrew chants and tried to emulate the other Jews around me. On Yom Kippur, the Day of Atonement, I fasted and repented of my sins. Yet I wondered why we could stand in the presence of God only *one* day a year. Although I sensed something was missing, I enjoyed the services.

After high school, my life revolved around the synagogue, my secretarial job, and my outside activities—which included taking a photography class at the local college. When I met Harry as a result of a class assignment, it was "love at first sight" (on my part, that is). However, it took Harry more than two months to make that first telephone call. After our first date, my mother warned me, "Leslie, marry your own kind!" I knew Harry was a Gentile—what I didn't know was that he was a *Christian.*

When we began dating, Harry explained to me how I could have a personal relationship with Jesus. I was intrigued by what he had to say and even went to church with him. But I confronted him with questions: If Jesus was who he said he was, wouldn't the Jewish people of his day have accepted him as their Messiah? If he was the answer to all of life's problems, why didn't more people accept him? Since I was Jewish and believed in God, what did I need Jesus for?

During the months we dated, we respected each other's beliefs—I went to church with Harry, and he went to synagogue with me. While I was hoping to convert him to Judaism, Harry was praying I would recognize Jesus as my Messiah.

After my sleepless night, I called Harry and asked him to come over. I *did* love him; maybe we could work something out.

When Harry arrived, we talked for a few minutes, not really having anything new to say. I was still adamant that I wanted nothing more to do with Jesus.

As a way of easing the tension, we decided to drive over to Harry's church and talk with the minister, who had become a friend of ours. Even though it was Saturday morning, we hoped the pastor would be there; however, when we tried the office door, we found it locked, and no one answered our knock.

Not knowing what to do next, we just stood there. At that moment, a stillness descended over me—I could no longer hear the sounds of the traffic going by. I felt completely engulfed in God's presence. His love surrounded me—awesome, warm, and reassuring. Suddenly, I *knew* Jesus was *my* Messiah, that he loved and died for *me*. No words were spoken—but in that moment, I moved from denial to belief. This time, there were no more doubts or questions.

One Sunday evening a few weeks later, Harry and I drove to the evening service at his church. When we got to the church parking lot, I decided I was ready to tell my parents I had accepted Jesus. Harry couldn't persuade me to wait until after the service, so he turned around and drove me back home. When he asked if I wanted him to go in with me, I told him I would do it by myself. Harry went back to the church.

Both my mom and dad were sitting in the living room. As I explained to them why I believed in Jesus, I thought, *Why, this is easier than I thought it would be—they may not fully comprehend what I'm saying, but at least they're not throwing me out of the house!* What I didn't know was that back at the church, Harry had slipped the pastor a note. In the middle of the service, the pastor asked the congregation to pray for a Jewish girl who was at that moment telling her parents she had become a Christian!

My parents didn't quite understand what had happened to me, but their basic attitude was "If Leslie is happy, then we're happy." Even so, my mother repeatedly questioned how I, a Jew, could do such a thing.

Although Harry and I were married by a Christian minister, our wedding was a blend of Jewish and Christian traditions. We were married under a canopy, which in Judaism symbolizes the home that is to be established. Harry even broke the traditional wine glass at the end of our wedding ceremony.

Harry's ways were not my ways when we married. We've had to learn to adjust to one another—and even after twenty-six years of marriage, we're still learning! But we keep Jewish traditions because Jesus' presence is found in them. Jesus is the Paschal Lamb of the Jewish Passover, the Indwelling Presence of the Feast of Tabernacles, the Light of the World celebrated in Chanukah.

Since the day I met Jesus, I've discovered I can trust him with every circumstance of my life. And I've learned that when I came to Christ, I wasn't giving up my Jewish heritage—by becoming a *completed* Jew, I was enriching it.

My Battle with
Breast Cancer

SHARON W. BETTERS

Suffering will come, trouble will come—that's part of life—a sign that you are alive. If you have no suffering and no trouble, the devil is taking it easy. You are in his hand.

Mother Teresa

S haron, the biopsy shows that you have cancer." Chuck, my husband, told me the grim news, his eyes filling with anguish. "The tumor has been growing in your breast for about two years. Dr. Warsall recommends a mastectomy and removal of the lymph nodes to determine if the cancer has spread."

I cried as the full impact of my husband's words sank in. How do we tell our children that their thirty-nine-year-old mother has cancer? Who would take it hardest? One of our three teenagers or ten-year-old Mark?

I apologized to Chuck for the tears rolling down my cheeks. It seemed crying was all I could do.

"I wish I could cry," Chuck said. "The pain I'm feeling might be released. So don't apologize for crying. When you cry, you cry for both of us."

All I knew about breast cancer was that if a woman lived for five years without a recurrence, she had a good chance of living a full life. Five years. Five years wasn't long enough, I told Chuck. Mark would only be in tenth grade. He would need his mother then as much as he needed me now.

Chuck went through every stage of this disease with me—diagnosis, surgery, even the "great unveiling" in the hospital. The presence of two nurses, a doctor, and my pride kept me from reacting emotionally to that moment. After all, I was a Christian; I believed the loss of a breast should be unimportant.

This attitude fueled my self-control until after my first shower at home, when I forced myself to look at my body in the mirror. Chuck found me sobbing uncontrollably over the ugly changes brought about by the surgeon's knife.

In my desire to be godly, I felt guilty because I experienced such grief over the loss of a breast. But Scripture reminded me that God places value on all parts of the human body. I concluded that the grief I felt was not ungodly but natural—and like all grief it needed time to subside.

At first, I felt no anger toward God. In fact, I felt as though God had wrapped me in a warm cocoon of love and security. I wish I could say I maintained that attitude. Still, God had "treasures of darkness, riches stored in secret places" to share with me, to show me that he was and is the Lord God (Isa. 45:3-5). I had to choose whether or not all I had been taught about faith and trust was true.

My anger spilled out after a visit to my surgeon and my oncologist following the surgery. The cancer had spread to my lymph nodes. The oncologist outlined a program of chemotherapy. I would enter the hospital for four days, once a month, for the next six months, to receive drugs intravenously. I hated the thought of needles and constant nausea.

Within a few weeks time, I was bloated from the medication and was losing my hair. *How could this have happened to me? I eat right, exercise, have regular checkups, and know of no family history of breast cancer. Why me?*

My angry words pounded on Chuck. I knew that God was sovereign in my life; I had trusted him with my welfare and believed he loved me. But since God could have protected me from cancer, I reasoned, he was the one responsible for my present circumstances.

Wisely, Chuck let me spew out all my bitterness. When I realized he was asking some of the same questions, I dared him to answer them. Instead, he pointed me to the Cross. He forced me to remember the faithfulness God had demonstrated to us in the past.

"Remember how hopeless our lives appeared before we were married and how you ran away from me because I wasn't a Christian?" he said. "Remember how God broke two rebellious teenagers and bonded us into a strong family?"

I reluctantly allowed the healing power of those memories to drip over the pain and bitterness in my soul.

I began to accept the fact that cancer had not invaded my body because of any personal sin but because of the corporate sin of mankind. I was subject to sickness simply because I lived in a fallen world. I could trust God to show me treasures in the darkness of cancer.

The expression of my anger was critical to inner healing. I never felt God's judgment, only patience and love as I worked through these emotions.

Scripture affirmed that my value is based on my relationship with Christ, not on any physical or personality trait. Baldness, bloating, and blue moods were my constant companions, yet so was God.

Medical studies have proven that the woman who has cultivated a deep joy in her life has a better chance for survival. Jesus Christ helped me to take a potentially disastrous set of circumstances and see the special joys. He brought smiles to my gloomy spirit as my eldest son would kiss me on the top of the head and say, "Kissing you is like kissing a baby—a bald baby." My twelve-year-old son admitted that the reason he could not go past me without giving me a hug was because his teacher told him everyone needs at least twelve hugs a day to live longer. His hugs were his contribution to my battle with cancer.

For the moment, I speak from a position of health. Aggressive treatments have squelched the cancer in my body, and my hair has grown back. I never forget that cancer is a vicious, devious disease. But whatever the future holds, cancer has not made me a victim. No, I am a victor.

Could Our Marriage Survive My Husband's Affairs?

A. M. Swanson*

*The names in the article, including that of the author, have been changed for privacy.

I have learned to see beyond
the physical reality in this
world to the spiritual reality.
We tend to think "life should
be fair because God is fair."
But God is not life. And if I
confuse God with the physical
reality of life—by expecting
constant good health, for
example—I set myself up for a
crashing disappointment.

Philip Yancey

The setting for some of life's most traumatic moments can be maddeningly ordinary. As my husband, Phil, and I sat opposite each other in our basement, he began confessing to sexual encounters with four other women during our seventeen-year marriage. Three had occurred before he had become a Christian, the last on a business trip to Las Vegas only four years ago. In each case, a prostitute was involved.

As tears coursed down his cheeks, Phil shared how heavy the burden of his adultery had become, yet how afraid he had been to tell me. Mechanically, I wiped his tears away as he spoke the words that forever changed our marriage. When he finished, we embraced, and somehow I mouthed, "Of course I forgive you. I love you." But it was as if someone else had pulled those words from my lips. At that moment I suddenly felt as though I were suffocating. Rage and horror filled me. *This can't be happening!* I thought. *How could he have treated my love so carelessly?*

So began our four-year journey toward healing that at times seemed doomed to fail. We realized almost immediately our need for help to work through this severe crisis in our marriage. Soon after his confession, Phil began seeing our pastor privately for counseling. He instructed Phil to spend one half hour each day talking to me about himself—his hopes, dreams, hurts from the past, his feelings for me and our marriage. Since I had always been the "talker" in our relationship, this was a tremendous growth experience for both of us.

As I learned to listen to Phil without interrupting, I discovered things about his past I had never been aware of previously. Phil's painful, insecure childhood made him wary of loving another person. As a lonely young man in the army, years before our marriage, he became involved with prostitutes—relationships that satisfied his lust without running the risk of emotional involvement.

Although he let his guard down after meeting and marrying me, when our marriage went through financial and health problems, Phil once again built walls to protect himself from pain. When a new job included regular overnight travel, the instability of our marriage led Phil to turn to prostitutes again.

To have kept his sin a secret from me would have spiritually crippled Phil. But its disclosure threatened to cripple me. Each day I tearfully confessed to God: "I *will* love Phil. I *choose* to forgive him." But in the darkest of nights, I slipped from our bed to weep because of the ugly, anguishing thoughts that engulfed me. During those lonely nights, I realized I had counted on Phil to meet all my needs. When I accepted Christ as my personal Savior several years into our marriage, Jesus had only been *added* to all I already treasured: Phil and our three children. In reality, Phil had been the most important person in my life. Now Jesus took his rightful place.

Despite Phil's and my progress over many months, our relationship was still strained. Ugly arguments erupted without warning. After one particularly volatile fight, I ran to a nearby park to be alone. As I wept, I picked up the Bible I had instinctively brought along. I opened the worn pages and my eyes fell upon Micah 4:9: "Why do you now cry aloud—have you no king? Has your counselor perished, that pain seizes you like that of a woman in labor?" It was as if God was telling me, *Amy, you are behaving as one who has no hope. You are wrong to despair like this. Always remember you indeed have a king—me.* From that day on, I vowed never again to display despair. I realized I had been refusing to cancel the debt Phil owed me for his unfaithfulness. When I returned home, I shared with Phil what God had revealed to me through the passage in Micah, and we forgave each other for the cruel words we had exchanged.

Phil also was being tutored by the Holy Spirit through the pages of God's Word. The words of Psalm 51, which poignantly reflect David's remorse over his adultery with Bathsheba, were seared into Phil's heart, becoming his own sincere plea before the Lord. He grieved to see how he had not only devastated me by his adultery but how he had sinned against God himself.

As our children matured, Phil shared with each of them the way God and I had forgiven him of his past moral failures. It provided a unique opportunity to share Christian guidelines regarding sexual conduct and to warn them of the painful effects of abandoning God's commands. All three of our children graciously forgave him, too.

One afternoon, while walking and listening to a worship tape, I thanked the Lord for his continued healing. Years had passed since the night my journey to forgiveness had begun, and the lessons learned were a bittersweet treasure. I thought of our upcoming twentieth anniversary. Phil and I planned to renew our marriage vows in a simple ceremony with only our three children present. I cheerfully asked Jesus to reveal to me a special gift I could give Phil—a gift he would know also was inspired by God's love for him.

Give him the gift of a bride's trust, the Lord quickly responded. I stopped cold. To completely trust again—as though the adulteries had never occurred—would make me vulnerable! How could I ever trust him the way I had as a young bride? "Oh Father! Help me!" I pleaded.

In the days that followed, the Lord showed me through Scripture how a bride trusts her bridegroom: She trusts when there is no track record of success. It is the kind of trust that caused Sarai to leave her family and follow Abram to Canaan, that enabled Abigail to mount a donkey and travel to David's side as he hid from Saul's wrath.

As I read 1 Corinthians 13:5-7, the familiar words took on a deeper meaning: "[Love] keeps no record of wrongs. . . . It always protects, always trusts, always hopes, always perseveres." I once heard a Christian conference speaker quote verse 5 and advise his audience to "fire your bookkeeper!" That's exactly what I had to do in order to give Phil his God-ordained gift. I had to release to God the record of wrongs stored in my heart.

Our anniversary arrived, and as we exchanged prayerfully written vows, our children witnessed the miracle of our resurrected marriage. How faithful God had been to preserve our family! As Phil vowed to be faithful to me, he slipped a new diamond ring on my finger. When he finished his vows, I held his hands and announced my own special gift to him: the trust of a bride. He was visibly moved by its significance. He knew God had graciously wiped the slate clean not only in heaven but also in my heart.

This May marks our twenty-fifth anniversary. Nearly a decade has passed since that night when our marriage was dealt a potentially lethal blow. By God's grace and the Holy Spirit's faithfulness, past failures no longer drown out God's gentle voice for our future together in him.

My Husband Lost His Faith

SARAH WEBER*

*The names in the article, including that of the author, have been changed for privacy.

*In God's faithfulness lies
eternal security.*

Corrie ten Boom

M ichael and I had been inseparable in college. We shared classes, study sessions, friends, and meals. We had met at a Friday night prayer-and-praise meeting and began dating. Our times together were spent sharing how Christ had changed us, especially Michael, who had been an active member of the late sixties counterculture.

Six months after our first meeting, we were married. Michael was preparing for the ministry, and I worked full time to support him. Five years later, Michael entered a small pastorate. We poured ourselves into the church. Our home was always open, even after the first of our three children came along. Yet, within six months, an elder in the church began to express dislike for some of Michael's ideas for growth. We stayed for two years, until one evening Michael looked at me and said, "I quit." I didn't protest.

Before long we had established ourselves with another denomination and started planting a church in a nearby community. I went back to work. But just as we began this new venture, we received a call from Michael's father that would forever change our lives.

"We can't come out for Thanksgiving," he said. "Your mother needs to have some tests at the hospital. She found a little lump underneath her arm." In ten months, she was dead.

And while we all grieved his mother's death, for Michael it was a crisis.

"Mom died angry and bitter with life and God. I'm not sure she even knew Christ. I just can't believe a woman who worked so hard and did so much good would not be in heaven," he told me.

Throughout the following year, Michael became increasingly depressed and bitter. He resigned from the church and began driving a bus full time. The more he kept himself from Christian friends, the church, and the Bible, the darker his life became.

Once an early riser to study the Bible and pray, Michael now slept as late as possible. Because of our conflicting work schedules, the children and I often didn't see him for days. His evening shift often stretched into the early hours of the morning as he unwound at a local bar. I watched in frustration as I witnessed Michael's character change drastically.

On Palm Sunday, nearly a year and a half after his mother's death, Michael opened up. Seated at the kitchen table, he cleared his throat and announced, "Christianity is a joke."

"What?" I asked. This was my husband, who had pastored a church. How could he say he didn't believe in God? I stared at him, my heart in my throat.

What followed were months of ups and downs. Both Michael and I fought periods of depression, frustration, and anger.

I finally shared with the pastor of the church I was now attending the shame I felt over Michael losing his faith. He listened attentively, then encouraged me to seek counseling.

Several weeks into counseling, my counselor suggested Michael join us. He agreed, and at our session I saw how sad, confused, and unsure Michael really was. Michael attended counseling for nearly two years, and although we didn't physically separate, we continued to grow emotionally distant.

Finally, I reached a point where I had to go one of two routes: stop believing in God as Michael had done, or challenge God to show me his goodness. I chose the latter, and the more I challenged God, the more goodness I saw. He brought Christian friends into my life when I needed them most, as well as providing the means to pay for my counseling.

As much as I wanted to hope things would change, I realized I couldn't change Michael. In his growing disbelief and anger, he often lashed out with comments like "Your Christianity is a fantasy, and your Christian friends are obnoxious, arrogant people."

I didn't want to give up my faith to save my marriage. But could I live with a husband who wanted nothing to do with my faith and constantly criticized it as well?

This past summer, Michael announced he no longer wanted to work on our marriage and would be moving out. I couldn't argue. Our fundamental values were now worlds apart.

One evening my pain gave way to a feeling of new strength. I can still picture it. I was folding laundry in the basement and sobbing. "After all we've been through! How can you just pull out?" I screamed into the empty basement. Then I said, "But I *can* make it without you." That insight was the beginning of great healing.

My life has not been easy since Michael left. I retain custody of our children and hold down a full-time job. Yet I find myself free from the stress of not knowing what to expect next. I look to 1 Corinthians 7:15 as a source of hope and comfort: "But if the unbeliever leaves, let him do so. A believing man or woman is not bound in such circumstances; God has called us to live in peace."

I think of Christ's words "Bless those who curse you" as I

continue to pray for Michael. Throughout this whole ordeal, my comfort has come from seeing God's faithfulness. I have told God my needs and seen him meet them one by one: supportive friends, counseling, or help budgeting my limited resources. While it hasn't been easy, it's always been clear what to do next.

With God's help, I am able to look forward with confidence to the new life he has prepared for me and my children.

My Daughter Is a Lesbian

KATHLEEN BREMMER
as told to CANDACE WALTERS

*Our human relationships are
the actual conditions in which
the ideal life of God is to be
exhibited.*

Oswald Chambers

When my daughter, Susan, invited me to lunch around Valentine's Day, I looked forward to chatting with her about her new job as a political consultant. Although we'd had our ups and downs in our forty years as mother and daughter, at that time, we were particularly close. Susan was quite late to the restaurant. When she finally arrived, I could tell something was wrong. Without much small talk, Susan abruptly announced, "Mom, there's something I've been meaning to tell you: I'm a lesbian." Her announcement absolutely stunned me.

I straightened my plate and silverware, avoiding eye contact with Susan. Then I picked up the menu and read it over and over, as if I hadn't heard what she had said.

"Mom, did you hear me?" Susan interrupted my trance.

"Yes, Susan, but you must be wrong," I stammered. "You can't be a lesbian . . . you've been married . . . besides, you're a Christian, and the Bible says it's a sin. . . ."

"Maybe your version of the Bible says that but not mine," she flatly stated. "Mom, you don't understand. It's like some people are born with blue eyes and some people are born with brown eyes."

Susan was defiant about her feelings, and I couldn't think clearly. Further conversation was impossible, so we left the restaurant without eating.

I tried to remember how to drive and where I lived as I found my way home in shock. I wondered how to break the news to Susan's stepfather, my husband of sixteen years. Before I could get the chance, he called for me to come quickly and see what was on the television. There was Susan on the news, being crowned "Miss Gay San Diego" and demonstrating in a gay-pride parade. We couldn't believe what we were seeing.

For weeks following my daughter's "coming out," I couldn't eat or sleep. I cried constantly. Hearing that Susan had died would have been easier to bear. It seemed all the dreams I had for my only child had been shattered. I didn't think I could continue to live, knowing my daughter was gay.

Our family was well known in the Christian community. It wasn't unusual to have my name in the paper as president of a Christian women's auxiliary or for my involvement in evangelistic crusades. So when our local newspaper covered Susan's involvement in the gay community, we received numerous phone calls from friends and acquaintances asking about her. Some callers were sympathetic, but most asked what we had done to cause her homosexuality. Other close friends were uncharacteristically silent. I couldn't talk to anybody. I was confused, embarrassed, and devastated.

At first, I began condemning myself. *Where had I gone wrong?* Like a mother who bandages a child's scrapes, I wanted to "fix" Susan, to pull her onto my lap as I did when she was little and correct any mistakes I might have made in raising her. I prayed, "Lord, just give me another chance."

I had always loved having a baby girl, dressing Susan in pink, frilly outfits trimmed in ribbons and lace. Susan's father died when she was quite young, and she was raised by my second husband—a prominent physician at a suburban hospital—until her teens. Unfortunately, he turned out to be a poor choice for a husband and father. He was unfaithful and abusive to me. Many years after my divorce, Susan told me he had sexually molested her from age five to thirteen. I had no idea this had happened to her and felt terribly guilty.

During adolescence, Susan was the typical "California girl"—blonde, tall, and slender. She was an excellent tennis player, a concert violinist, and an honor student. She was offered a full music scholarship to college upon completion of high school but instead chose to marry a boy she had met on the tennis courts. Unfortunately, her husband was killed in an automobile accident during their second year of marriage.

Following her husband's death, Susan started college. It was there, I believe, she began a lesbian relationship with a classmate. Once I found a note from one of Susan's girlfriends that seemed overly affectionate, but in those days I didn't make the connection.

I didn't understand much about homosexuality eleven years ago. Although I was repulsed by it, I suddenly had to confront it in my own daughter's life.

One day, when I was at my lowest and the pain seemed unbearable, I met with Barbara Johnson, author of *Where Does a Mother Go to Resign?* Her book chronicles her struggle to cope with her son's homosexuality. Barbara explained that homosexuality is a condition with such deep and diverse causes that no mother should hold herself responsible for "making another person gay." God knows I made plenty of mistakes in parenting—and I'm sure, as with many lesbians, Susan's sexual abuse was a contributing factor. But homosexual behavior is first and foremost an individual's choice.

Barbara stressed how important it was to be in a support group with other parents and loved ones of homosexuals. I couldn't find such a group, so I started one in San Diego that has met every Tuesday night for the past eleven years. In talking with hundreds of other hurting moms and dads, we have been mutually helped and encouraged by the belief that Jesus Christ can defuse any darkness in our children's lives. I also co-organized an annual conference that features nationally known experts who help those struggling with homosexuality and teach others how to minister to homosexuals and persons with AIDS.

In the years since Susan told me she is a lesbian, she has been quite active in the gay community. At one time she was the publisher of a gay newspaper. Now Susan travels the country lobbying for homosexual rights on behalf of an influential gay political caucus. She and her companion own a home on the East Coast.

We talk by phone nearly every week, and Susan sends me cards with lovely floral designs she says remind her of me. She knows about my support group and conferences and has even attended one of the workshops. It doesn't help to give Susan Christian tapes or books about homosexuality; she knows what the Bible says and how I feel about her sexual orientation. She interprets the Bible differently, so we get nowhere discussing it. Sometimes I still lovingly confront her, but she understands that my love and approval are two separate things.

When Susan visits me, we sample a favorite seafood restaurant at the beach or a Mexican one in Old Town San Diego. I just want to be with Susan as a mother, not as an adversary. I feel it's vital to grasp the moment—I may not have another chance to love her. I've seen too many parents lose that chance forever by cutting off all contact with their gay son or daughter.

I know that God is bigger than homosexuality. All I can do is give Susan to God. I cannot change her—only God can. Susan has chosen this path, and I must allow her to accept responsibility for her own actions. My role is to be Susan's intercessor, on my knees praying for her and trusting God for the outcome.

Legacy of Love

JANE LANDIN RAMIREZ

*Didst thou give me this
inescapable loneliness so that
it would be easier for me to
give thee all?*

Dag Hammarskjöld

It was an early October morning—and as usual, I rushed about to get our second grader, Kevin, and fifth grader, Joe, ready for school and myself ready for work. Since my husband, Sandy, had the morning off, he was busy making breakfast for everyone.

"Daddy, can you take us to school today?" asked Kevin.

"'Fraid not, Bunbun. Your daddy's gonna work off some pounds today on his bike." He turned to me and winked his right eye (our silent way of saying *I love you*). "I want that new suit your mom bought me to fit just right."

Sandy had just been promoted to assistant manager at work, and we were all proud of him. "Don't forget, I'm taking my special girl out tonight for a celebration dinner," he added.

Sandy had always been a romantic. He had won my heart our freshman year in high school with his homemade valentine, and twenty years later, he could still make me blush.

Before leaving, Kevin hugged Sandy and reminded him to buy him a new eraser for school.

"'Bye, Dad, be careful on your bike," added Joe, as we walked out to the car.

"See you soon! I love you," Sandy said, waving to us from the front door.

I dropped the boys off at school and hurried to the office. My morning was so busy, I decided to work through lunch. *Nothing's going to keep me from leaving on time today!* I thought.

But shortly before three o'clock, a coworker and close friend, Rose, entered my office. "Jane, there's been an accident," she said, ashen faced. "Sandy's at the hospital."

"How bad is it? Why didn't someone call me? What hospital is he at? Who called you?" I asked, panic-stricken.

"Calm down, Jane. I don't know how badly he's hurt. His boss called me. Someone from the hospital called him. I'll drive you there," she said.

Rose dropped me off at the emergency entrance and left to park the car. I was sure everyone around me could hear my heart pounding against my chest as I went up to the front desk and asked to see my husband.

The emergency room attendant telephoned someone. "His wife is here," he said quietly, then turned to me. "Someone is coming to talk to you. Please wait here."

"Is he all right? Where is he? Can I see him?"

"Please wait here, ma'am. Someone will be here soon," he pleaded.

The hospital chaplain arrived and quietly ushered me into a private waiting room. "Mrs. Martinez*, your husband's been with us since nine-thirty this morning. We were told by the ambulance attendants he was hit by a car while riding a bicycle. The doctor will be here soon to talk to you. Is there someone I could call for you?"

This is a bad dream—I'll wake up from it soon, I thought, dazed and speechless. Just then, Rose entered the room. Her worried face triggered the tears I was fighting back. She sat me down

*The author has since remarried.

and took over calling my family and our pastor. "Your sister is bringing the boys," she said.

I jumped to my feet when the doctor entered the room. "Mrs. Martinez, I'm Dr. Gray. Your husband is in ICU. I'm afraid the news isn't good. He suffered severe trauma to the head and spine. We had to amputate his left leg to control the bleeding. He's not breathing on his own, and the blood supply to his brain is about 2 percent of the normal level. His injuries were so severe, it's a miracle he's hung on as long as he has. I'm sorry—there's nothing more we can do."

My legs collapsed. I had to be helped to a chair. Anger and guilt consumed me, and I lashed out, "He's been alone all this time! Why did you wait so long to call me?"

The chaplain responded, "Mrs. Martinez, your husband wasn't carrying any ID, so the police only had the initials from his high school ring to go on. One of our nurses identified him from the yearbook and remembered where he worked. His boss told us he would try to locate you. I'm sorry it took so long to contact you," he said, retrieving a small cloth bag from his coat pocket. "Here are some of his personal belongings."

It contained a crushed class ring, a bloodstained wedding band, our house key, a broken wristwatch the boys had given him for Father's Day that displayed the time of 9:08, and a pink eraser with Kevin's name on it. It was as if Sandy had been stripped of all ties to us.

As I carefully placed the small bag into my dress pocket, the lump in my throat finally let my words escape, "Please take me to him."

"He never regained consciousness. His injuries have distorted his features, and all the tubing going through his body may be shocking," explained Dr. Gray.

"I need to see him right now," I insisted.

I followed Dr. Gray. Tears welled in my eyes as I approached Sandy. I caressed his cold hands and gently kissed his forehead. "I'm here, my love. I'm so sorry that I didn't get here sooner," I said softly. Thoughts raced through my mind: *I'm so afraid—I don't know if I can go on without Sandy. I feel so alone. Please help me, Lord. Why did this have to happen? I feel so helpless. Dear God, please spare him any further suffering. Lord, help me to be strong for the boys.*

Suddenly, a twitch in Sandy's right eyelid interrupted the serenity of his face. "I love you, too," I whispered. "You're in God's hands now." I so wanted him to open his eyes and hear him tell me everything would be all right.

Our silence was broken by a tap on my shoulder. Dr. Gray asked me to follow him. Outside the room were two other people.

"Mrs. Martinez, I know this is an extremely difficult time for you," said Dr. Gray. "I wish there were an easier way to do this, but there's very little time. Your husband's heart and other vital organs weren't injured by the accident, and there are two people here from an organ bank. They'd like a few minutes with you."

"Please, Dr. Gray, are you sure there's no hope? Didn't you see his right eyelid move?"

He sympathetically replied, "I wish I could tell you what you want to hear, but the movement of his eyelid was simply a reflex motion. Please listen to what these people have to say."

I had never given organ donation any serious thought. Sandy and I had never discussed it, and the idea was a bit frightening. But I listened as they gently asked me if we'd consider the possibility of donating Sandy's organs. Everything was happening so fast that I was relieved to see our pastor arrive.

Reverend O'Connor followed me into Sandy's room. "Sandy isn't going to make it, and those people you saw were talking to me about donating his organs. I don't know what to do," I said.

"Jane, Sandy's work in the church exemplified his caring, giving nature. Remembering that may help you decide what to do. It's a decision, however, you shouldn't make alone. Do the boys know what's happening?" he added.

"No, they're on their way. I don't know how I'm going to explain all of this to them," I said as we both returned to the waiting room.

The crowded waiting room became a silent blur of faces when I entered the room. Two frightened little boys raced to me.

"Where's Daddy, Mommy? Why can't we see him?" they both asked.

I led them by the hand to Sandy's room. They stared at the figure on the bed as if he were a stranger. "Daddy is very hurt. He was struck by a car and thrown from his bike. He hit his head very hard. Don't be afraid."

Kevin moved a little closer to the bed and touched his father's hand. "Daddy," he said, "your little Bunbun is here, and I'm going to help you get all better."

Hot tears rolled down my cheeks.

Joe pulled on my arm. "Is Daddy going to die, Mommy?"

We all huddled in a tight embrace, and I began, "Boys, the doctors have done everything to try to help him. We all love him very much, and I know you both want him to get better."

"Yes, Mommy, but how can we help him?" asked Kevin.

"The doctors can't help him, and we can't help him, but there is someone who can help him," I said.

"You mean God, don't you, Mommy?" asked Joe.

"Yes, God can help him, but to do that, he needs to take Daddy to heaven to live with him," I answered.

"But then we won't see him anymore, like Grandpa," sobbed Kevin.

"Daddy will always be with us, Kevin. He is in our hearts, and it's because we love him so much that we need to let him go to heaven where he won't hurt anymore. Grandpa is already in heaven, so Daddy won't be alone there. Someday, when we go to heaven, we'll see both of them again," I explained.

"Do you remember how Daddy was always helping other people?" I added.

"Yes, Daddy liked helping people, even people he didn't know," added Kevin.

"Do you think Daddy would want to continue helping people if he could?" I asked.

"I guess so, but how, Mommy?" asked Joe.

"In heaven, God will take care of Daddy and he will give him a new body that doesn't hurt. Daddy won't need his old body anymore. There are people right here that we could help feel better if we gave them Daddy's beautiful green eyes or his great big heart," I explained.

"Will Daddy still love us even if he doesn't have his old heart? Will he still remember us?" questioned Kevin.

"Of course he will. Daddy will always love us no matter what happens," I answered.

After a brief silence, Kevin spoke, "Let's help those people, Mommy. Daddy would want us to."

Joe remained silent a few minutes longer. Cuddling his father's hand between his two small hands, he gently kissed it and whispered, "I love you, Daddy. Tell Grandpa I love him, too." Then he quietly slipped out of the room.

The rest of the family supported our decision without hesitation. My cold hands trembled as I signed the consent papers. After giving all the family some quick time alone with Sandy, the surgeons went to work to save all the organs possible.

My numb body was oblivious to the chilly October breeze that greeted us when we left the hospital about seven o'clock. As my sister drove me home, I thought of the celebration dinner that would never be and the new suit that would now be worn for the first and last time.

The healing process that followed was made easier with each letter we received from an organ bank. Although the identities of the recipients were concealed, one wrote about the high school principal with a failing heart who was within hours of dying until he received Sandy's heart. We heard from the kidney foundation about the two persons who were now free from their dialysis machines. Two elderly persons received the gift of sight through cornea transplants. Sharing the letters with Kevin and Joe made it easier to talk about our loss.

Two months after the accident, we faced our first Christmas without Sandy.

"Mommy, who's gonna put our Christmas lights up this year?" Kevin repeatedly asked.

I knew I couldn't disappoint the boys and break a family tradition of decorating our home with Christmas lights, but I just couldn't get into the Christmas spirit. Then it came—a letter from the tissue organ bank. As I read it aloud, the boys listened intently: "Your generous gift of life has shed light on the lives of some one hundred burn patients and their families, some with very severe skin burns. . . ."

"Mom, Daddy's been gone a long time, and he's still helping people," Joe said proudly.

"Mommy, I don't think that letter is right. Daddy was a very big man. I can't believe he only helped one hundred people. He probably helped at least a million!" Kevin added.

Memories of past Christmases flashed through my mind. Sandy always played Santa at our family gatherings. The old Santa suit didn't need much padding, and his naturally jolly cheeks and *ho ho ho*s brought laughter to all. He would be missed deeply—particularly this first Christmas—and not only by his family. There'd be one less volunteer this year to deliver food and gifts to the needy on Christmas morning. The people from the Ronald McDonald house, where he served guests hot meals every other Friday evening, had already expressed how much he was missed. And the beautiful sympathy card made and signed by the students from his Sunday school class reflected the love they had for their teacher. One child had written, "I am not going to be sad because Mr. Martinez always made me laugh."

Christmas is a joyous season, I reflected. Like the child from his class, I, too, would refuse to be sad. Sandy had touched the lives of many—and even now his legacy of helping others was very much alive. I could not—and would not—let him down.

With renewed invigoration, I exclaimed, "Boys, what do you say we get started on those lights and make Daddy proud of us, too!"

A Heart Prepared for Thanksgiving

JONNA CLARK

Acceptance says, "This is my situation at the moment. I'll look unblinkingly at the reality of it. But I'll also open my hands to willingly accept whatever a loving Father sends."

Catherine Marshall

I t was the week before Thanksgiving, and as I was driving through town running errands with my three sons— Benjamin, six; John, two; and Ethan, four months—I tuned in to a broadcast of Dr. James Dobson's *Focus on the Family* radio program. The guest that day was talking about the death of her child, so I flipped the radio off, not wanting to hear—let alone think—about the subject.

But my thoughts seemed to have a life of their own. *What would I do?* I pondered halfheartedly. As I mentally prepared my grocery list, the answer came in the voice I've grown to recognize as my heavenly Father's: *Jonna, you'll get down on your knees and thank me for your child and for every moment, every day you were given.*

That's strange, I thought, tucking the thought away in some corner of my mind as I drove on into the happy clutter of my life.

One week later, my husband, Patrick, our three boys, and I gathered to celebrate Thanksgiving at Patrick's parents' house three hours away. While a football game buzzed in the background, numerous siblings and their burgeoning families arrived laden with hugs and special dishes.

How blessed we are, I thought, relishing the warmth of the fireplace, the delicious aromas filling the air, and the joy of seeing Patrick's grandmother holding baby Ethan for the first time. Ethan smiled and burbled as family members snapped his picture and oohed-and-aahed over him.

Eventually I whisked Ethan away from the hubbub of last-minute meal preparations and the noise only a large, happy family can make and efficiently laid him down on his back for his nap on my in-laws' bed. I adjusted the covers, settling him quickly and quietly without so much as a backward glance.

After we thanked the Lord and enjoyed our feast, I went to the bedroom to check on Ethan. Instead of finding him napping, he was lying facedown and motionless. My heart skipped a beat as I snatched him from the bed.

"Ethan!" I screamed, jostling him to awaken him. But when he didn't respond, fear took over and animated my wooden legs. I raced into the kitchen, holding his limp body. Screaming for Patrick, I yelled, "Dial 911! Ethan's not breathing!" My mother-in-law cried out in disbelief as family members familiar with CPR took him from me and began resuscitation attempts.

By that time I was utterly beside myself with a mind-numbing combination of panic and pain. When the paramedics arrived and began to work over his still, little form, I pulled myself together enough to begin begging God for Ethan's life. Within minutes, a Med-Flight helicopter landed in the street outside to take Ethan away to a nearby hospital while Patrick and I raced there by car.

During that car ride, my begging ended. I still clung to hope that Ethan would be revived, but as I prayed in the back seat with my sister-in-law, I remembered what had happened the week before when I had listened to the Dobson program. My heart breaking, I thanked God for every day we had been given with Ethan and prayed for God's will to be done.

Once at the hospital, we learned that the team of doctors and nurses had tried their best to bring him back, to no avail.

Ethan had died of Sudden Infant Death Syndrome—SIDS—well before the helicopter had taken him away. Twenty minutes after our arrival, Ethan's IV lines were removed and the life-support machines turned off. Weeping, Patrick and I held Ethan's lifeless body. At last, after prayer and time with the hospital chaplain, we left the hospital and our baby's body to return to Patrick's parents' home in a state of deep shock and anguish. Our family held us and cried, not knowing what to say or how to help. The worst call I've made in my life was to my family to tell them the news. We also asked our pastor to begin funeral arrangements.

At some point, I went to the bathroom to be alone for a moment to calm my racing pulse and runaway thoughts. As I slumped on the edge of the bathtub, I wished I were dead instead of Ethan. Life loomed ahead of me desolate and unfathomable. I felt as though I stood on the edge of an abyss into which the slightest breeze would send me toppling.

It was then I heard my loving Father speak again: *Be still, and know that I am God.* Immediately I calmed, sensing his presence.

Since that moment, I've grappled mightily with what Ethan's death means, but for those first, horrendous hours, God held me close in the knowledge that he was there, that I had not been forsaken.

We've marked many a mile in our journey through grief and mourning since that Thanksgiving Day four years ago. It hasn't always been one of revelation and comfort. At first, I was filled with guilt, consumed by the thought that I could have prevented Ethan's death. I've since learned that SIDS isn't anyone's fault. It strikes roughly one in a thousand babies and most likely has something to do with brain-stem abnormalities and other factors still largely unknown to experts.

There have been times when I railed against God, my friends, and family as I tried to make sense of the loss. Times when I refused to go on with life without Ethan—and lashed out at those who were trying to continue with living.

That first Christmas after Ethan's death, the lights and decorations, even cards and letters, evoked nothing but disgust in me. All expressions of joy hurt. The first Easter I sat on my bed, still in my pajamas well into the day, screaming over the phone in raw anger at my mother because she had the audacity to want to plan a gathering.

There were occasions when I thought I would welcome the release of death, if only to escape the numbing cold of deep-down depression. I realized I needed the help of other moms who had experienced this, so I joined a SIDS support group to help me work through my sorrow.

But while others in my SIDS support group seemed able to move through their grief, I remained wounded and afraid I might never fully recover. It was at that point I chose to see a Christian counselor, and it was the greatest investment I've ever made.

As I spent the next eighteen months working through the loss of Ethan, I came to understand that the death of a loved one—especially a child—shakes us to our very core. I learned, through the process, that God not only prepares us for brokenness but uses it to teach us some invaluable lessons if we allow him. And I came to know patience, for nothing and no one can hurry grief. I ultimately grew up and into my faith, for it's only when we face painful loss that we truly discover the meaning of *Thy will be done.*

I'll never be grateful for death and loss, but I'm thankful for the ways in which Ethan's life and death have changed me.

Before his death, I rushed to the next activity, purchase, phase, or place. I was so hurried that I never fully enjoyed the present. Now I can spend an afternoon pulling weeds and tending the flowers or patiently guiding the small, clumsy hand of a child intent on mastering simple but time-consuming needlework. I've slowed down, given up worrying as a pastime, and learned to let go.

Corrie ten Boom, author of *The Hiding Place*, survived a Nazi death camp after sheltering Jews in her home during World War II. Later, when she spoke about the experience, she urged her audience to hold things in life loosely enough that they wouldn't be irreparably broken if those things were wrenched from their grasp.

Today I strive for that lighter, looser grip on life and those I care for. I've learned that in life there's only one guarantee—Jesus. No one can bring Ethan back or "fix" the situation, but in Christ I've found healing and restoration.

My Children Exposed My Prejudice

ANITA PRINZING
as told to EDWARD GILBREATH

*Skin colour does not matter
to God, for he is looking upon
the heart. When men are
standing at the foot of the
cross there are no racial
barriers.*

Billy Graham

It was going to be a Christmas to remember. Our oldest son, Mark, a marine private, was stationed in England, and our other two children (Debby, a senior in college, and Scott, a senior in high school) were about to make my husband, Fred, and me official empty nesters.

I thought it'd be wonderful if we could all celebrate the holiday together—in England. Fred, who was then a pastor of a large Baptist congregation in Portland, Oregon, agreed.

My usual holiday anticipation took on added significance. I pictured us in Dickens's London with carolers singing under streetlights in the freshly fallen snow. It wasn't long after our arrival in England, however, that my picture-perfect Christmas fantasy unraveled.

Since Mark seldom wrote us letters, we didn't know much about his life at the military base—if he'd made many friends or found a church to attend. Fred and I were filled with pride when we first saw Mark, arrayed in his marine attire. *Our son is all grown up,* I thought. However, parents' intuition alerted us that something was bothering him. Realizing that prying would probably do more harm than good, Fred and I patiently waited for Mark to tell us what it was.

A few days later, Mark dropped his bombshell. "I'm dating

a woman I met at the base here," he told us. "And let's just say Grandad wouldn't approve." He didn't need to say anything else. Mark was dating a black woman! Our glaring silence betrayed our stunned disappointment.

We returned to the States a few days later, thinking that time and distance would take care of the situation—Mark was returning to the States in March and would be assigned to a different base.

During the next few months, we heard little from Mark. However, at about five-thirty one Sunday morning, the telephone awakened us. It was Mark calling from England. After exchanging greetings, he said simply, "I called to let you know I'm getting married to Martha, the woman I told you I was dating. Do we have your blessing? Can you come to our wedding this June in Louisiana, where Martha's from?"

We were totally unprepared for Mark's news. With just a few words, our family dream of finding what we considered the "perfect" mate for each child was erased. We'd never discussed the choice of a marriage partner with our kids other than to stress the importance of selecting a Christian. Suddenly we wished we'd been more specific.

Thinking we were open-minded, we'd exposed our kids to missionaries, foreign students, and people of different ethnic backgrounds. Yet, when it came time for our son to choose a mate, we weren't even remotely ready for his selection.

After the initial shock wore off, Fred and I had to ask ourselves, *Why do we have such a hard time with the prospect of our son marrying interracially?* Mark's fiancée, Martha, was a Christian, so what was the matter? Did the problem lie with Mark and Martha—or with us?

I'd prided myself that I wasn't prejudiced like my parents. My mother had come from the South, and although she'd loved her "mammy" (her family's African American domestic helper), her family had never allowed the woman to sit at their dining table. And my father, although a loving man to his family, was Archie Bunker in the flesh. Now, as I faced the prospect of my son marrying a black woman, I realized I harbored many of the same feelings as my parents.

For years I'd prayed God would bring the right person for each of our children—but I couldn't believe this was his will! I became angry with God. Why did I even think of entrusting him with the job if this was what he was going to do?

I wrestled with the situation for several weeks. Finally, I tried praying about it, but because of my anger with God, I wasn't getting very far. One evening, after Fred had gone to bed, I was reading in Colossians. I cried out to God, "I have to have something. I've either got to accept this and have peace about it, or I'm just going to throw up my hands and quit!"

Just as I was pleading for peace, God answered me in a passage of Scripture: "You are living a brand new kind of life that is continually learning more and more of what is right, and trying constantly to be more and more like Christ who created this new life within you. In this new life one's nationality or race or education or social position is unimportant; such things mean nothing. Whether a person has Christ is what matters, and he is equally available to all" (Col. 3:10-11, TLB). Reading that verse didn't change the reality of my situation, nor did it immediately erase my ingrained prejudices; however, it gave me some peace to accept what God was doing and to trust him for what lay ahead.

That June 19 was one of the longest days of our lives. It was a beautiful wedding, held outdoors under a sweltering Louisiana sky. Although we were happy for Mark and Martha, we were also overwhelmed by the emotion of everything that had transpired during the previous six months.

It was no longer a question of whether or not Mark and

Martha should get married. They *were* married. Nothing would change that fact. We could either accept their marriage or allow it to cause us anguish.

It became undeniably clear that the Lord was trying to teach us something when that August, just two months after Mark and Martha's wedding, our daughter, Debby, surprised us with the news that she had begun dating an African American man. Still adjusting to Mark's marriage, Fred and I stared at each other in disbelief.

We soon found that Debby's friend, Bruce, was a fine young man. He was a Christian with a good education and a promising career as a lawyer. His interests and goals seemed similar to Debby's. Once again, we had to admit, our major concern was race.

Two years later, Debby and Bruce were married. Theologically and theoretically, Fred and I had no reason not to approve of Debby and Bruce's marriage. But emotionally and spiritually, we were still dealing with our prejudices and stereotypes.

There we were, a pastoral couple who addressed all types of family and emotional issues in our ministry to others—yet when it came to the subject of interracial marriage, we felt as though we were in no-man's-land. There were few people we knew who were grappling with the issue as we were.

My guarded quest to share my struggle with others made me feel like a turtle tucked in her shell, timidly poking her head out to test the safety of her surroundings. I had a friend whose son was engaged to an Asian girl, so I asked her how she was dealing with accepting a daughter-in-law of another background. She said unwittingly, "Oh, I don't have any problem with that, but if she had been black, I would have." I immediately pulled back into my shell. In the eyes of some of my friends, marrying someone of another race was the worst thing our kids could have done to us.

Yet, God slowly showed Fred and me that people of different races marry for the same reason two white people or two black people marry—for love. Our children had married people they loved. And once we got to know our daughter-in-law and son-in-law as individuals, we also learned to love them.

Mark and Martha were stationed in another part of the country, so we couldn't get together often. But it was easy to like Martha—she was a shy but sweet young woman. As we spent more time together, she admitted to being terrified when we first met. Not only were we in-laws, she said, we were *white* in-laws. As we grew more sensitive to her feelings, we began to place her name first ("Dear Martha and Mark") in each letter we wrote them and made a point of talking with her each time we called. We didn't want to give Martha any reason to think she held a lesser place in our hearts.

After the arrival of our three grandchildren, it became even more apparent to us that love isn't a matter of race. A few years ago, Fred was spending an afternoon with Mark and Martha's daughter, Marquis, who was then four years old. As they labored together on a coloring book, Fred asked her, "What color is Grampa?" Marquis said, "White." Then he asked, "What color is Marquis?" She replied, "Black and white." Finally Fred asked her, "What's your *favorite* color?" Without hesitation, Marquis answered, "Purple and pink."

The color of a person's skin wasn't an issue with Marquis. And through our experiences, God has taught us that because of Christ, it should no longer be an issue for us, either.

As our relationships with our children and their spouses have grown stronger, we've all found a new freedom to express ourselves more openly. During a recent visit, Martha asked me something she'd wanted to know for a long time.

"Mom," she said, "were you more concerned with my skin color or my rural Southern background when Mark and I wanted to be married?"

I knew I had to be honest. "Martha," I began carefully, "I'm ashamed to admit this, but it was only your skin color that bothered me."

Martha was surprised. "I always thought it was my background," she said.

That conversation never could have taken place during the first few years of our acquaintance. Despite our differences, we are growing closer as a family. Today, Fred and I can sincerely say we are proud of our children and their choices of a marriage partner. The apostle Paul set forth a Christian perspective on interracial marriage when he said, "From now on we regard no one from a worldly point of view" (2 Cor. 5:16). When we allow ourselves to see people from *God's* viewpoint, their skin color and cultural differences become secondary to their character and immeasurable worth in his sight.

I'm Living with AIDS

DAWN WOLFF
as told to MARIAN V. LIAUTAUD

*O*nly in the fellowship of
suffering will we know Jesus.
We identify with him at the
point of his deepest
humiliation. The cross, symbol
of his greatest suffering,
becomes our personal
touch-point with the Lord of
the universe.

Joni Eareckson Tada

When my doctor called me in November to schedule an appointment to go over the results of my recent medical tests, I knew the news was bad. For more than two years I had struggled with bouts of pneumonia, bronchitis, abdominal pain, and severe fatigue. Since the birth of my second son, Nile, my health had continued to deteriorate, and several physicians had deduced I was suffering from Chronic Fatigue Syndrome. I thought my doctor was going to tell me I had lupus and that it would be difficult to treat lupus and CFS together. But when he told me I was HIV positive, I was shocked.

Nile, then three and a half, was with me when the doctor gave me the test results. As we waited in the reception area for copies of my medical records, he looked at me with questioning eyes as tears streamed down my face. All I could think of was, *Nile, you're so young. Will you even remember me after I die?*

I spent that first afternoon crying and praying. When my mom came home, I threw my lab results down on the counter. She looked at it and said, "What does this mean?"

"It means I have AIDS." We hugged each other and cried.

I called my estranged husband, John, to tell him about the test results. Since our separation that June, I had learned of his involvement with other women during our marriage. Now I wanted to know how many women he had been with. Several months later, I also learned from a friend that although John had told me he had never used IV drugs, he admitted to her husband that he had used them during his navy years. Almost worse than finding out I was HIV positive was discovering that the nine and a half years I had been married to this man had been a lie.

I confronted John with his behavior, but he denied the possibility that he could have infected me, even after he tested HIV positive himself.

Getting John to take responsibility for my illness was futile. Rather than harbor anger at him, I turned to God to find a way to turn a bad situation into something positive.

The boys were scheduled to visit their dad that weekend, so I used the time alone to come to grips with my diagnosis. I stayed up most of the night crying, reading my Bible, and praying for the strength to face this ordeal. Then I came across Matthew 15:28: "Then Jesus answered, 'Woman, you have great faith! Your request is granted.'"

I knew this wasn't the end of my tears—but I also knew God would be with me through every hardship I would face. "Thank you, God," I wrote in my journal, "that I know you will never give me a burden that's too heavy for me to carry. I especially pray, dear Lord, for those around me who still suffer far worse than I. They will see me suffer physically and feel helpless to stop it. When I die, they must continue on, while I will be with you. Whether I live a few more months or a few more years, please give me the strength to get through this ordeal."

That same night, I also wrote letters to Nile and Sean, my six-year-old, to be given to them upon my death. Since I wasn't sure how much longer I would live, I wrote at their current level of understanding. We had recently seen the movie *The Land before Time,* in which a little dinosaur loses his mother. I explained to them that even though Little Foot couldn't be with his mother, he could still talk to her, think about her, and feel her presence. In the same way, I told them, I would always be there for them in spirit. I also encouraged them to remember to turn to God for everything.

After I finished the letters, I felt a sense of peace. I knew God would help me over every hurdle I would have to overcome. Little did I know how difficult the obstacles would be.

The following week, I reluctantly received my first flu vaccination to protect me from becoming sick. My body reacted negatively to it, and I ended up in the emergency room with severe nausea and dehydration. I also had an allergic reaction to the antibiotic I was taking for bronchitis and was covered with hives. This was the first of many late-night trips to the hospital.

At the same time, I was anxiously awaiting the results of my sons' HIV tests. Because the doctors couldn't pinpoint exactly when I became infected, they felt it best to determine whether or not the boys were carrying the virus. Sean's results came back first—they were negative. But there was a holdup on Nile's test. My mind swung from hoping he would test negative to knowing he was infected.

Early in December—one month after my diagnosis—I learned what I feared most—Nile also was HIV positive. I didn't know what to hope for—that he would die first so I could be there for him or that I would go first so I wouldn't have to watch my baby die.

When I told my immediate family about Nile and me, they had mixed reactions. My family had no problem with being around me, but they did not want Nile to play with his cousins for fear of transmission. With Christmas just around the corner, this came as a severe blow. A few days before the holidays, however, my brother called to say we would be welcome for the family Christmas get-together. He and his wife had done some studying on AIDS and learned they would not be at risk by mere exposure to us. Having my family's acceptance was the best Christmas present I could possibly have received!

My parents have relied heavily on their faith for support. But unfortunately, neither they nor I received the help with this trauma we needed from our church. Our minister was simply unable to get beyond the word *AIDS*. In fact, he agreed with my mother that we should hide behind the disguise of a different diagnosis. For months, we told people I had leukemia. I was touched by the compassion and gifts we were showered with—yet I wondered, *Would they respond the same way if they knew the truth?* I felt as though I were living a lie. I kept telling myself, *I didn't do anything to deserve this disease. Why should I have to lie about it? Christ didn't turn away those who were sick—so won't others accept us regardless of what we are sick with or how we got it?*

In February, the boys and I moved from my parents' home into our own apartment.

We also found a new church where I felt free to share our suffering. The congregation had already experienced an AIDS death in their membership, so they understood our struggles and needs. There I've felt a real sense of acceptance and compassion.

Many times, God's provision has come in the form of a person offering help exactly when we needed it most. Last fall, I became gravely ill at a time when we were without a caregiver for my sons. Our church passed around a sign-up list, and people volunteered to bring meals and watch the kids. A volunteer from the Milwaukee AIDS Project watched my boys for several hours until he got them to bed so I wouldn't have to wake up. He called the next day to let me know how the boys did and offered to remain a regular volunteer, assisting me with the boys a few nights a week. Since then, he has become a close friend and wonderful role model for my boys.

Having AIDS has given me a forum within the church to help Christians consider what their response to people with HIV/AIDS should be. I also devote time and energy to speaking at schools about AIDS awareness and prevention. I know God didn't cause this disease to happen to me. But I *do* believe he has called me to use my abilities to write and speak so people can put a face with the disease. Before I speak, I always pray, "Dear Lord, let the words from my mouth be your words and not mine. Lead me to say what these people need to hear today."

Sometimes it feels as though AIDS is one big fight. It's bad enough we have to fight for our lives. But every day is a struggle to get up and maintain normalcy for myself and the boys. The hardest thing for Sean has been not having friends over to play. We used to have a houseful of kids over, but these days I'm usually too tired or sick to oversee the boys while they're playing.

But while I may not be able to take Sean and Nile sledding or to basketball games, I can still tell them how much I love them. I still have the final say on what movies they watch, what activities they can go to, what discipline is appropriate. And I have placed people in our lives who help me maintain our home, care for them, and keep close tabs on our medical, emotional, and spiritual well-being.

Doctors hesitate to speculate on my life span. One day I can be doing relatively well. Then, within twenty-four hours, I can be in the hospital wondering if it's time for me to relinquish custody of Sean and Nile and become institutionalized. Two summers ago, I went through a terrible time when I lost the use of my extremities and had difficulty understanding what people were saying to me. My pain was so severe, I remember praying to God just to let me die quickly or give me relief.

My health has continued to go downhill, though I am basically stable and have never had an opportunistic infection. But whenever the pain gets to be too much, I lie in bed and picture myself basking in the warmth of Christ's love. At times, during severe pain, I have felt myself lifted into Christ's arms to be comforted.

As for Nile, he was diagnosed with a full-blown case of AIDS when he was four and a half. Today, two years later, he continues to have monthly drug infusions to help boost his immune system. Sometimes he throws tantrums and sends his medicine flying across the room, screaming, "I'll die if I take my medicine."

I have been open with my kids about the fact that I will eventually die from AIDS, and Nile is aware that he, too, faces the same future. He has a lot of pent-up anger over having AIDS, but he's a fighter. He talks about heaven as a place where people aren't sick anymore and knows he'll see his mom there someday.

Sometimes, when I watch my sons sleeping peacefully or playing, I wonder how my death will affect them. How will they adjust? What else should I be doing now to help them cope with their loss? Will they resent the fact that they don't have two living parents? I have tried to instill in them the knowledge that God is with them, watching over them in every situation, so they know they are never alone.

The most difficult issue facing me now is coping with the fact that my parents will probably end up raising my kids. I feel a mom should be there for her kids—and I won't be. I have a hard time with that.

But I will not be defeated. Even though AIDS is a dreadful disease, it has helped me stay focused on the Lord instead of earthly things. And as we struggle to live with AIDS, we learn daily the extent to which Christ is the source of our strength.

Gambling to Lose

Maxi Chambers*

*The names in the article, including that of the author, have been changed for privacy.

True love is not a feeling by which we are overwhelmed. It is a committed, thoughtful decision.

M. Scott Peck

I pushed the last of my red chips toward the dealer and tried to smile. But as he slowly turned over the cards, I knew I had lost the last of the ten thousand dollars I had desperately borrowed.

"Better luck next time!" the dealer shouted, trying to cheer me up. I quickly turned so he wouldn't see the tears streaming down my face. I was thirty thousand dollars in debt, my twenty-year marriage was nearly destroyed, and my four children no longer respected or trusted me. I had hit rock bottom.

The neon lights of the casino shined brightly in the midnight sky as I left to get into my car. I turned back for one final look at a building that represented what had become my obsession during the past three years. The realization of what I had lost—and what I had become—sank in.

I had become a compulsive gambler whose only thoughts were on placing a bet, playing bingo, or shooting the dice. Three years ago, my faith and my family had been the most important things in my life. An elected city council member, successful owner of a hairstyling business, and activist who organized youth groups and volunteered at the local schools, I was well known for my Christian values and my boldness in proclaiming Christ. But I had abandoned God's input in my life and pushed my husband and children aside so I could indulge in my addiction.

As I drove the fifty miles home, I wept uncontrollably. All the excuses I'd used to justify my habit seemed lame. There were no more people or banks to borrow from, no more words to use to manipulate my husband. I begged God to forgive me, to help me overcome a compulsion that had become more important to me than he was.

My gambling addiction began with a simple game of bingo. I had seen a building sign advertising it, so out of curiosity I went in and played. That first time, I won five hundred dollars. It seemed so effortless! Since my husband, David, and I had been having some financial problems, the money was like a gift from God. I was able to pay some bills and even purchase a few extra things. When I told David about my winnings, he seemed equally happy, so I took his smile of approval as an OK to play again.

Even though I was a Christian, I didn't realize gambling was wrong. I'd never heard a sermon preached against it, other than a few words by a former minister who warned against "playing too much lottery." Since I viewed myself as a disciplined person, I didn't think I'd ever have a problem.

At first, every win was wonderful. My heart pounded, adrenaline pumped, and I literally shook with excitement. I never had to deal with the hassles of life at the bingo parlor. There were no harassing phone calls from unhappy citizens, no children to demand my time—only the need to concentrate on my bingo cards and listen for the next number to be called.

Over the course of a year, what began as a once-a-week activity developed into an every-night event. David, who worked long hours, didn't realize the extent of my involvement, but my children, ages eighteen, seventeen, fourteen, and twelve, did. To ease my guilt about spending so much time away from home, I'd vow not to go next week. But all my promises to stay home were always forgotten.

If my guilt became too intense, I'd rationalize my behavior: *Don't I deserve a night away from the kids? Besides, if David didn't work so much, I probably wouldn't be doing this. I need the companionship.*

As my playing time increased, so did my debt. At first, I asked David for money to gamble with, but soon he began to object. To get him to give me the money, I'd make him feel guilty about working so much. If that didn't work, I'd use the promise of sex or lash out in anger. Eventually, David handed over the money, a hundred here, two hundred there. Bills went unpaid—yet I gambled on.

David was ashamed and hurt by my behavior, so he began to withdraw almost completely from our home. This only intensified my loneliness, and our relationship started to deteriorate.

As my debt grew, so did my desperation. I started looking for other forms of gambling in the hopes of "hitting it big." I found an advertisement for a new place to gamble—a nearby Indian reservation where the winnings were supposedly bigger. With every trip to the grocery store, I'd purchase twenty or thirty dollars' worth of lottery tickets. At the bingo parlor, I'd not only play the regular games but spend hundreds of dollars on "pull-tabs." I even remember spending more than four hundred dollars for the chance to win two hundred and fifty.

David became increasingly agitated about my habit, so to avoid pushing him too far, I began to borrow money from friends and acquaintances, always providing them with a good reason why I needed the money. Because of my reputation, they always lent it to me without question. But while they were congenial, David was not. Every evening that he came home before I went to bed was an evening filled with angry words, promises, and tears.

My sisters and parents stepped in to fill the void in my children's lives. But while they were of great support, each of my children showed signs of emotional wounding. Our oldest child became withdrawn, our second son, rebellious. Our two youngest children cried often and became severely depressed. Because I often used the money for necessities for gambling instead, they went without new shoes, clothes, or even sometimes a warm meal. Instead, I delayed each purchase until the bitter end, hoping to win the money to buy whatever they needed.

Two years into my gambling, I began to feel suicidal. I cried constantly, seldom slept, and didn't know a single minute of mental peace. My doctor began treating me with both tranquilizers for sleep and antidepressants.

Even though my life was a mess, I still maintained the persona of a successful, ethical person. Local merchants who ordinarily wouldn't cash checks did so for me because of my reputation. But as the checks became larger and my losses greater, I was forced to find other ways to finance my habit. I started funneling the money I needed from my hairstyling business, and since its checking account was only in my name, I could manipulate money to cover my spending without David's knowledge.

As my sisters and family became increasingly aware of my gambling, they confronted me. "You have a problem, Maxi. Please get some help," they pleaded.

"I'll go with you to Gamblers Anonymous," said another. "I'll even drive."

But while I knew my family was right, not only did I not want to stop, but I feared the consequences of stopping—getting caught and facing my creditors.

During the last few months of my gambling, a riverboat casino came to a town near us. The casino's bright lights and music appealed to me, and I quickly became a regular. In fact, I was one of the first to obtain VIP status.

It's easy to lose hundreds, thousands, even more in a casino. Whether you're playing blackjack, slots, craps, or roulette, it's all designed to make the casino rich—and the player poor. The more I went, the more my debts mounted, and before long, I thought of suicide constantly.

By this time, I had more than two thousand dollars in outstanding checks. I knew that if I didn't find some money fast, I could go to jail. David refused to give me any more money; he had already borrowed from everyone we knew. We had signed for two loans from different banks, and he had on at least two occasions sought out money from professional loan sharks. I didn't dare ask him for anything.

Instead, I called a local savings and loan company and convinced them to allow me to apply for money over the phone and then take the loan papers to David to sign. David never saw those papers—I forged his name and used the ten thousand dollars to cover what I had already spent. The rest I lost that night at the casino.

As I cried out to God, I knew I had to do something. I could either give in to my suicidal thoughts or choose life. I chose to stop my behavior and rebuild my marriage and my relationship with my children.

I knew this decision meant having to confess some things I didn't want to. And it meant facing the full extent of my family's frustration and anger. But by the time I reached my house, I felt the first inklings of peace since my addiction had begun.

The next morning, I cleaned the house of anything that

spoke of gambling. I also sat down with my checkbook, totaled my damages, and approached my extended family with one final request for a loan. They gave me a small amount of money that gave me some breathing room for a few more days to get myself together.

The following day, I began to shake from withdrawal. Even the thought of gambling made me anxious. I decided I needed to keep busy, so I called my pastor and asked to see him. Upon our visit I confessed what was happening with me and asked if I could do some volunteer work for the church.

That same evening, I called my children together and asked for their forgiveness. I reassured them that with God's help, I could overcome my compulsive behavior. It was a wonderful time of sharing, but I knew my actions would have to prove my words.

Almost two weeks passed, and I knew I still had one more major thing to do: I had to tell David about the ten thousand dollars. I asked him to spend the morning with me instead of going to work. It was the first time in our marriage he'd ever stayed home even half a day from his job.

There's no doubt David's long hours at work contributed to my gambling addiction. I was lonely and felt isolated. Dealing with three teens and one preteen is stressful enough, but alone it is very hard. Instead of facing these situations, gambling had been my escape. As David listened for the first time in our relationship, I told him the truth about myself and acknowledged responsibility for my actions.

As the hours passed, we talked about the children, my fears of future struggles, and our financial situation. We discussed David's hurt and his frustration. Then, when he began to speak about money, I stopped him. The time had come.

"David," I said. "I have something to tell you."

I could see his body tense as he searched my eyes for some

sense of what I was going to say. I began to cry as I said, "You have every reason to divorce me. No one would have put up with what you have endured over the last three years. You and the children have been through more pain than anyone should have to suffer. There are no excuses for what I'm about to tell you." Then I told him about the ten thousand dollars and the forgery.

When I finished, David sat stunned and silent. I waited anxiously for his next words.

"I love you," he said, as he wrapped his arms around me and hugged me tightly. This time I didn't cry alone. David and I wept for the pain we both had endured, for our children, and for the love we'd nearly destroyed by our selfish ways. And we wept for turning to our own lusts for money and self-satisfaction instead of to God.

Over the next few months, David and I worked hard to change. He came home earlier more often, and I became more vocal about my needs. I began to structure my days so I'd be busy during the times I'd normally gamble. I asked my best friend to help "talk me through" any withdrawal I felt.

God didn't deliver me from my urge to gamble instantly. For weeks, gambling constantly filled my thoughts. I dreamed about playing bingo or standing in a casino. Even to this day, I awake in a cold sweat from these nightmares. But the dreams come less often now, and I'm thankful I'm no longer on any drugs for depression or sleeplessness.

My recovery has been slow and methodical. So has the resolution of my financial mess. God didn't send thousands of dollars to my doorstep to solve my financial crisis, nor did he wipe away the balance due my creditors. But what he did do was send some unexpected work my way and give me the assurance that everything would work together for good. Although God forgives, we reap what we sow—and I've had to suffer the repercussions of my misconduct. I've had to work hard in reestablishing my credibility in my most intimate relationships.

Today, my relationship with God is growing. And every day that I resist temptation, I feel a little stronger. I no longer avoid church out of fear of feeling guilty, nor do I refuse to pick up the Word for fear I'll read something too convicting. Now God's Word comforts me and confirms my hope that through Christ, I can overcome.

David and I went out for breakfast recently. As we walked by a newsstand, I glanced at the headline of the early morning paper: "Gambling Blamed for Young Mother's Suicide."

I bought the paper, and David and I read it together as we waited for the waitress to take our order. The details of this young woman's story were almost identical to mine—except that rather than face the fact that her house was being taken away because of nonpayment due to her gambling debts, this mother of two had shot herself.

I wept as I thought of the hopelessness this young woman must have felt. Gambling—and the potential it carries to destroy lives—is all too familiar to us. But restoration is no longer something only hoped for. Thankfully, with God's help, it's become a reality.

Hope in the Midst
of Infertility

MARY ROBERTS CLARK

*Answers aren't the real
issue. Clinging to God
through all of life's
circumstances and helping
others to do the same—that's
what's important. Life's
lessons never end—we can
either gain wisdom and
understanding from them or
let them beat us down. It's a
daily choice.*

Bernadette Keaggy

My husband, Al, and I glanced at the magazines in my gynecologist's office as we waited for her to come in. I'd already read a lot about infertility and had promised myself I'd never go through the tests I'd read about. Now I was willing to go through anything.

When Al and I married, I had already waited thirty-nine years for God to give me the husband of his choice. Having been single for so many years, I thought God had taught me all there was to learn about patience and trust in him. So on that sunny June day when we exchanged vows, I just *knew* God would give us a child right away—especially at my age. There was no way he would make me wait!

But by the following June, I'd been through twelve months of ecstatic hopes and devastating disappointments. After each cycle ended, I promised myself I wouldn't get my hopes up again. But a week later, I'd find myself consumed with how high my temperature had climbed. (Basal body temperature helps detect the most fertile days each month.)

The next two weeks would bring emotional highs and lows. I'd mentally decorate the nursery or stroll longingly through the infant department in my favorite store. But each month, the day of truth arrived and yanked me back to reality.

I shared my pain with friends, but few understood. Many of

them had become pregnant the first month they tried. Their attitude gave me the impression that I must be doing something wrong.

Others had experienced infertility but had finally conceived or adopted. Their pain was so far in the past, they'd forgotten it. Just adopt, they'd admonish with a grin as their toddler pulled on them.

One or two friends were experiencing the same problem, then they became pregnant and were afraid to tell me. They had no idea how much it hurt to hear their good news through the grapevine. Didn't they realize I could be happy for them? I wondered. Did they think I was that selfish?

When nine months had passed, I called several adoption agencies. The first one had so many couples on their waiting list, they no longer were accepting applications. The second had a seven-year waiting list and would be glad to send us information—though the thought of adopting a child at age forty-seven made me gasp! Another required that you be married at least three years. I stuffed the information in a file and put the thought of adoption on hold.

My prayer group prayed—at first. Boldly they went before the Lord to request a baby for us. With joy they thanked God for the special bundle of joy he was going to send our way. But after a year—and still no pregnancy—our prayer group looked embarrassed. I could tell they didn't want to talk about it anymore. After all, they'd prayed and nothing had happened. My husband and I felt guilty for even requesting prayer—other people's problems were bigger, anyway.

My doctor finally came into the room and sat across from Al and me.

"We don't need to look at *that*," she said, flipping over a magazine. *That* was the picture of a newborn on the cover; she didn't want Al and me to have to look at a baby while we talked about my inability to conceive. How was she to know that picture of a baby gave me hope, and her gesture of kindness made me feel like an even bigger failure?

Al and I went through all the tests over the next two months, the ones I never thought I'd have to undergo. They tested my blood for everything from luteinizing hormone to progesterone. I had dye injected through my uterus and tubes, and Al gallantly suffered through semen analysis.

None of our tests showed any abnormalities. But nothing happened. I didn't become pregnant by taking my temperature every morning before getting out of bed. I didn't become pregnant by using an ovulation predictor kit each cycle. I didn't become pregnant—no matter what we did!

And so, each month, Al and I waited. I denied every sign that I wasn't pregnant and imagined every one that I was. Each month, when my period arrived, I cried tears of anguish, mourning for the child I felt I lost, the child that had existed only in my imagination.

Al held me as I sobbed. He hated to see me hurt. But his faith was so much stronger than mine. "God will give us a baby in his time," he'd tenderly remind me.

Then I'd dry my tears, pray, and try to surrender. But within days, the routine would begin all over again: hope, excitement, anticipation . . . denial, despair, grief.

As friends began to encourage me to trust God and get involved in other things, I'd occasionally recall a verse I memorized years ago: "Give thanks in all circumstances, for this is God's will for you in Christ Jesus" (1 Thess. 5:18).

As an act of my will, I began to thank God for infertility. I wasn't thankful for the delay or for my broken heart. I wasn't thankful for the tests we'd been through. But because I knew God's plan for me is best, I was able to say, "Thank you, Lord, for not giving us a baby yet."

That's when God began to bring positive circumstances into my life. For several Sundays at church, I had felt he wanted me to help out in the nursery. I resisted the leading. Let the mothers keep the nursery; that had always been my motto. But one Sunday, I could no longer resist and waited anxiously for the sermon to end so I could talk to the nursery coordinator. (Needless to say, she almost cried tears of joy when I volunteered!)

Soon after I took that small step of obedience, our church's Christian school asked me to become a volunteer. I've been able to work in a setting that affects many children.

I'm reminded of God's promise in Isaiah 54:1:"'Sing, O barren woman, you who never bore a child; burst into song, shout for joy, you who were never in labor; because more are the children of the desolate woman than of her who has a husband,' says the Lord." The Lord hasn't left me alone in my infertility—he's filled my empty arms with many beautiful children.

When I was finally able to surrender to God my strong desire for a child, he gave me peace. Al and I still hope to have a baby someday, but in the meantime, I've learned I can trust God's timing after all.

Faith in the Face of Recession

ANNIE OETH

*S*tars may be seen from the
bottom of a deep well when
they cannot be discerned from
the top of a mountain.

Charles H. Spurgeon

My husband and I were living the American Dream—and we never thought it would end. We had a three-bedroom house in the suburbs, membership in the area's most exclusive country club, two cars, and plenty of plastic credit at our disposal. If I wanted a new dress or handbag, I bought it without hesitation. Since my husband, a regional sales manager with a large corporation, traveled about five days a week, a trip to the mall also eased the loneliness I felt. Neither of us liked his extensive business travel, but we liked what his paychecks could buy—the opportunity for me to stay home and care for our two young sons, and a seemingly secure future—complete with college educations for our children and a retirement of leisure. We thought we had it all.

But one January morning, I heard the unexpected sound of my husband walking down the hall. I knew he was supposed to have left on a four-day business trip.

"What'd you forget, hon?" I called. When our eyes met, I knew something had shaken him.

"I had a meeting at the office early. They just laid me off." His lips trembled. His job level was being eliminated, and he and another regional sales manager were out of a job.

I was shocked. He had been with the company for more than thirteen years, and his work had always been exemplary.

So this is how they pay us back, I thought, shock changing into anger. *They haven't just laid off some nameless, faceless statistic to trim the company budget—they have laid off my husband and my family!*

"Why is this happening?" I wanted to scream at God. *Layoffs happen to others but not to hardworking Christian men like my husband,* I thought—as though being a Christian was a ticket to financial prosperity. A hatred for those who had decided my husband's fate lodged deep in my heart and wouldn't budge.

As the recession deepened and the months passed, I felt myself becoming even more frightened and discouraged. Our savings dwindled, and there were no job prospects on the horizon. My husband had good days and bad days. On good days, he would have breakfast, shower, and scan trade and business publications, searching for a job, or call old friends in his field, hoping they would know of an opening. When tired of job hunting, he would play with the kids, go fishing, or fix something around the house. But on bad days, he stayed in bed past noon, let his face stubble grow, and watched television all afternoon and into the night. While I went through the routine of caring for our children, cooking, and cleaning, I could feel myself being drained by worry over our financial situation and my husband's depression and anger toward his former employer.

However, one day, while reading Proverbs 31, my eyes hit on a verse in the chapter before: "Give me neither poverty nor riches, but give me only my daily bread. Otherwise, I may have too much and disown you and say, 'Who is the Lord?'" (Prov. 30:8-9). I recalled the times God had provided manna for the Israelites as they wandered in the desert. He had given them just enough to meet their daily needs and strengthen their faith.

God is using this career pitfall to call our family closer to him! I suddenly realized. *This layoff is part of his plan. If we look for them, we'll see God's blessings.* The anger I had felt toward my husband's boss began to melt. I asked God to forgive me for my worry and impatience toward my husband. I even prayed for those who had ordered my husband's layoff. And I found myself able to see some of the blessings God was giving us that my self-pity and anger had obscured.

For the first time in our marriage, my husband and I had plenty of time to spend together. We started taking walks and stayed up late to talk. Our oldest boy became his father's shadow, following him and imitating him whenever possible. My husband was able to watch his boys grow up day by day, something he had missed when he was traveling and earning a large salary.

Socializing used to mean dinner out with friends. Now we stayed home and had much livelier evenings playing heated matches of Trivial Pursuit with other couples.

And my husband was able to spend precious time with his father, who was dying of cancer. He had asked his employer for time off to visit his father, but the request had been denied. This, too, was a gift from God, for they would not have had that time together unless the layoff had occurred.

The experience of being a laid-off family was a blessing in many other ways. I learned to care more for others. Prior to the layoff, I had little sympathy for the unemployed or homeless. Now when I watch the evening news and see footage on the homeless, I think, *There but for the grace of God goes my family.*

God saw beyond what we had wanted. Instead, he gave us what he wanted us to have. And that, I've come to learn, is far better than anything we could want for ourselves.

In November, my husband found work at a company that encourages family values and appreciates his efforts. He enjoys his new job much more than the old one. It is a joy for me to see him excited about going to work. And best of all, once our move to a new city is complete, we'll be home together in the evening to share a real family life, something that was almost nonexistent with his previous job.

I've discovered we have something much better than the American Dream—a God who loves us and guides us to true spiritual prosperity.

ACKNOWLEDGMENTS

Today's Christian Woman magazine and Tyndale House Publishers would like to thank the following people who graciously gave their permission to use the following material first in *Today's Christian Woman* and now in *Amazing Love.*

Betters, Sharon W. "My Battle with Breast Cancer" (July/August 1990).

Bloedorn, Angie, as told to Una McManus. "My Daughter Was Conceived in Rape" (May/June 1994).

Bremmer, Kathleen, as told to Candace Walters. "My Daughter Is a Lesbian" (January/February 1994).

Brook, Linda Rios, as told to Diane Eble. "Forced to Choose" (September/October 1992).

Brooks, C. C. "I Had to Fall in Love with My Husband . . . Again" (January/February 1995).

Cavano, Joyce. "Honoring My Father" (September/October 1996).

Chambers, Maxi. "Gambling to Lose" (November/December 1996).

Chisholm, Gloria. "I Couldn't Love My Mother" (January/February 1992).

Clark, Jonna. "A Heart Prepared for Thanksgiving" (November/December 1996).

Clark, Mary Roberts. "Hope in the Midst of Infertility" (March/April 1994).

Clausen, Marie. "The Most Terrifying Night of My Life" (September/October 1991).

Cleland, Ann, as told to Camerin J. Courtney. "Life after the Flood" (July/August 1994).

Craig, Debra M., as told to Marian V. Liautaud. "The Day after Father's Day" (May/June 1992).

Eldridge, Sherrie. "In Search of My Birth Mother" (May/June 1993).

Lescheid, Helen Grace. "My Prayers Went Unanswered" (September/October 1993).

Liautaud, Marian V. "I Was a Prisoner of Panic Attacks" (July/August 1991).

Lindsey, Ruth Crawford. "Please, God, Not Alzheimer's" (January/February 1996).

Miles, Christine. "The Day the Hurricane Hit" (July/August 1993).

Malloy, Kathleen, as told to Holly G. Miller. "My Husband Forgave My Unfaithfulness" (January/February 1997).

Oeth, Annie. "Faith in the Face of Recession" (July/August 1992).

Prinzing, Anita, as told to Edward Gilbreath. "My Children Exposed My Prejudice" (November/December 1994).

Ramirez, Jane Landin. "Legacy of Love" (November/December 1995).

Strom, Kay Marshall. "Up in Flames" (May/June 1991).

Swanson, A. M. "Could Our Marriage Survive My Husband's Affairs?" (March/April 1992).

Weber, Sarah. "My Husband Lost His Faith" (March/April 1991).

Wolff, Dawn, as told to Marian V. Liautaud. "I'm Living with AIDS" (November/December 1992).

Wright, Leslie Shapiro. "My Messiah, Too" (March/April 1993).